Palgrave Macmillan Studies in F
Intimate Life

Series editors
Graham Allan
Keele University
Keele, UK

Lynn Jamieson
University of Edinburgh
Edinburgh, UK

David H.J. Morgan
University of Manchester
Manchester, UK

'The Palgrave Macmillan Studies in Family and Intimate Life series is impressive and contemporary in its themes and approaches'
—Professor Deborah Chambers, Newcastle University, UK, and author of *New Social Ties.*

The remit of the Palgrave Macmillan Studies in Family and Intimate Life series is to publish major texts, monographs and edited collections focusing broadly on the sociological exploration of intimate relationships and family organization. The series covers a wide range of topics such as partnership, marriage, parenting, domestic arrangements, kinship, demographic change, intergenerational ties, life course transitions, step-families, gay and lesbian relationships, lone-parent households, and also non-familial intimate relationships such as friendships and includes works by leading figures in the field, in the UK and internationally, and aims to contribute to continue publishing influential and prize-winning research.

More information about this series at
http://www.springer.com/series/14676

Jacqui Gabb • Janet Fink

Couple Relationships in the 21st Century

Research, Policy, Practice

palgrave
macmillan

Jacqui Gabb
Faculty of Arts and Social Sciences
Open University
Milton Keynes, UK

Janet Fink
University of Huddersfield
Huddersfield, UK

Palgrave Macmillan Studies in Family and Intimate Life
ISBN 978-3-319-59697-6   ISBN 978-3-319-59698-3   (eBook)
DOI 10.1007/978-3-319-59698-3

Library of Congress Control Number: 2017948663

Cover design by Tom Howey

Printed on acid-free paper

This Palgrave Macmillan imprint is published by Springer Nature
The registered company is Springer International Publishing AG
The registered company address is: Gewerbestrasse 11, 6330 Cham, Switzerland

Foreword

What are the everyday lives and experiences of couples in Britain today? How has the changing political and economic zeitgeist of these contemporary times impacted on couple relationships? What are the resiliencies, strengths and resources that couples bring to their relationships and that help them to endure? How do differences in experiences of gender, generation and parenthood impact on understandings of couple relationships? These contexts, interactions and relationships in society are mirrored in our consulting rooms—microcosms of happenings in the wider world. Thus, much of what couples and families bring to therapy nowadays has to do with Internet-related problems, addictions and affairs; fears of racism and invidious xenophobia; gendered inversions to the household as the financial crisis results in women becoming primary breadwinners; and the impact of forced migration on family and couple relationships.

As a practising couples and family systemic psychotherapist, meeting couples in the consulting room, I reflect on the above issues on an almost daily basis. Yet when I look to the academic literature, there is a paucity of research that addresses the challenges and dilemmas faced by couples in Britain today. This seminal text, based on the mixed methods study *Enduring Love? Couple Relationships in the 21st Century*, makes a crucial contribution, therefore, to scholarly research by providing a rich and detailed exploration of themes for contemporary couple-ness and the social and political contexts in which couples live out their lives. This is important for clinicians because, as one of the pioneers of systemic psychotherapy, Gregory Bateson (1979: 15) has argued: 'Without context, words and actions have no meaning at all.' As such, this book has shaped and informed my practice, and I believe that it speaks to all clinicians, regardless of their modality, not least because so many of the themes and methods have direct clinical relevance.

First and foremost is the idea of relationship practices, the quotidian rituals of couple and family life that preserve and strengthen couple bonds and nurture intimacy. In my consulting room, I am always curious about the ordinary actions that couples engage in, and how they negotiate their time spent together and apart. The examples included in this book shed light on what goes on behind closed doors and the everyday-relationship dynamic; they paint in vibrant colours couples' creative use of activities that are imbued with personal, couple and cultural meanings. I am moved by the reciprocal acts of kindness and generosity that partners will extend to each other even when their couple relationship is under threat.

Nonverbal acts and gestures are embedded in couples' everyday lives and are captured through the innovative graphic research method of emotion maps that were used in the *Enduring Love?* study. Devised by Jacqui Gabb in the early 2000s, emotion maps use spatial and visual metaphors to map out family relationships. The emotion map method has been successfully imported into systemic psychotherapy (Gabb and Singh, 2015), helping to open up family communication and bring a situated account of everyday parent-child and couple interactions into the therapy room. The technique has also been further taken up and extended by clinicians and researchers, helping to explore intercultural couple relationships (Singh, 2017), children's experiences of domestic violence (Callaghan, Alexander, Sixsmith and Fellin, 2015; Alexander, Callaghan, Sixsmith and Fellin, 2015) and parent-adolescent interactions in South Africa (Koen, 2017).

Another highly significant theme is what the authors describe as 'unsettling coupledom'. This has to do with the diversity of lived couple relationships and how couple relationships are constructed and understood differently in different cultures. We all carry a template or blueprint— informed by our own families' of origin and culture—about how couple relationships ought to be, and about what constitutes a 'good couple'.

However, as Winterson, (2017) argues, we need to be more imaginative about modern marriage and not presuppose permanence. Myths and fairy tales often draw on the notion of finding one's soul mate and living 'happily ever after', a notion that continues to saturate contemporary culture but which does not reflect the complexity of experiences of 'coupledom' in contemporary times. This book unsettles the conflation of myth and lived lives; research data is used to illustrate the ways that couples may be situated within heteronormative convention that predicates 'the one' but *in practice* their lived experience is far richer. Couple relationships draw on a range of significant others to support the partnership and to ensure that the relationship remains individually fulfilling.

In our clinics and consulting rooms, we increasingly see diverse couple forms, including step families, transgendered couples, and polyamorous relationships. We also see more intercultural couples than ever before, which may well reflect a changing trend in Britain, where one in ten relationships is intercultural (ONS, 2014). Interestingly, a quarter of the couples interviewed in the *Enduring Love?* study were intercultural and talked about their experiences of profound racism and resistance to their unions, and in collaboration with Jacqui Gabb, I have reflected on some of the key issues associated with researching racial diversity and working with intercultural couples (Gabb and Singh, 2014). In my clinical practice with intercultural couples, I am reminded of the resiliencies in the relationships of the intercultural research sample, which included: protection from racism, allowing a synergy of both languages and cultures, the importance of a mixed-race community and media representations of mixed-race families (Singh, 2014).

As therapists, we perhaps need to be attentive to the risk of privileging talking cures and verbal communication amongst couples. The book illustrates, for example, a range of vivid accounts about how couples communicate, highlighting the value of verbal communication as well as the power of silence. It also demonstrates how couples use technology and social media to communicate; for example, texting was used to negotiate practicalities, practice intimacy, express emotional closeness and mediate the relationship. In some cases, texting was felt to be a safer and less intrusive way to communicate than through phone conversations or face to face. At other points, e-flirting and sexting facilitated couple intimacy and operated as a facilitating precursor to embodied sexual intimacy or as virtual means of reconnection and 'touching base'.

There has been much recent media interest in increasing awareness about mental health. Although the book is based on a non-clinical sample, there were inevitably some participants in the *Enduring Love?* study who experienced mental health difficulties. Couples therapists and counsellors often encounter couples where one or both live with mental health issues but need to know more about how these issues affect relationships. What are the resiliencies and strengths of relationships where couples stay together and care for each other through such difficulties? How would clinicians work with couples where one or both suffer from mental health difficulties? These are some questions that would be of interest to clinicians and clinical researchers and that may, hopefully, be addressed in further research from the study! However, as it stands, this wonderful book has much to offer those of us who work at the frontline with couples in the twenty-first century.

Dr Reenee Singh
Founding Director, London Intercultural Couples Centre and
Co-Director, Tavistock Family Therapy and Systemic Research Centre

References

Alexander, J. H., Callaghan, J. E., Sixsmith J., & Fellin, L. C. (2015). Children's Corporeal Agency and Use of Space in Situations of Domestic Violence. *Living Reference Work Entry. Play, Recreation, Health and Wellbeing,* 523–543.

Bateson, Gregory. (1979). *Mind and Nature: A Necessary Unity.* New York: Dutton.

Callaghan, J. E., Alexander, J. H., Sixsmith, J., & Fellin, L. C. (2015). Beyond 'Witnessing'. Children's Experiences of Domestic Violence and Abuse. *Journal of Interpersonal Violence.* doi: 10.1177/0886260515618946

Gabb J., & Singh, R. (2014). Reflections on the Challenges of Understanding Racial, Cultural and Sexual Differences in Couple Relationship Research. *Journal of Family Therapy,* *37*(2), 210–227.

Gabb, J., & Singh, R. (2015). The Uses of Emotion Maps in Research and Clinical Practice with Families and Couples: Methodological Innovation and Critical Inquiry. *Family Process, 54*, 185–197.

Singh, R. (2014). Love Across Border Control. *Media Diversified,* 5 February.

Singh, R. (2017). Intimate Strangers? Working with Interfaith Couples and Families. *Australian and New Zealand Journal of Family Therapy,* *38*(1), 7–14.

Winterson, J. (2017). We Need to be More Imaginative about Modern Marriage. *The Guardian,* Saturday, April 8.

Preface

Politics and policy

Since the initial publication of *Couple Relationships in the 21ˢᵗ Century* and the completion of the *Enduring Love?* study that underpinned our analysis in this book, there have been major shifts in the UK's political landscape, not least the 2016 referendum vote (Brexit) to leave the European Union (EU), and a seeming rise in populism, protectionism and anti-immigration (Clarke and Newman, 2017; Holbort, 2016; Jessop, 2016) that is similarly reflected in the 2016 election of Donald Trump as president of the United States. While much debate about Brexit has been focused on its manifestation of the social divisions within UK society and its potential impact on UK trade, there are also growing concerns about how it will affect the personal relationships and welfare entitlements of EU migrants living in the UK and UK migrants living in other EU Member States (Currie, 2016). Over 3 million EU migrants currently live in the UK and 1.2 million UK citizens live elsewhere in the EU which means that Brexit has brought an unprecedented layer of complexity and precarity to intercultural cross-national relationships. EU migrants living in the UK face an uncertain future and their associated couple relationships are in a state of limbo as they negotiate their own future citizenship and residency rights and those of their children

(Guardian 2017). This has generated a huge surge in the numbers of people seeking to gain UK residency (Guardian 2016a), with considerable financial costs being incurred by individuals in their applications for settlement and naturalisation (Gov.UK 2016). The emotional strain this puts on couples is much harder to calculate, although Resolution, the UK's largest family law organisation, has reported that the stress of Brexit has compounded pressure on couples already on the cusp of divorce (Guardian 2016b). Relationship support services have begun to report a significant increase in Brexit-related arguments that feature during counselling. For example, a survey completed by Relate, the UK's largest provider of relationship support, indicated that arguments over Brexit were feeding into partners' sense of difference from one another, leading to questioning of their shared beliefs and values (Independent 2016a). As we discuss in more detail later in this book, sharing values, beliefs and interests with their partner is experienced by couples as a key 'connector' in their relationship, enabling them to overcome other external stressors that might otherwise place the relationship under duress. It is not surprising, therefore, that the palpable precarity amongst intercultural couples following Brexit has led frontline services to demand that we pay sufficient attention to the emotional consequences of these contemporary political contexts (Singh and Dada 2017).

Moreover, arguably the most prescient point of this shifting political landscape is its continued neo-liberal political impetus, which means that it is not only UK-EU couples who are immediately affected by the Brexit vote. It is forecast that leaving the EU will result in a reduction of the household income by 6–10%, equating to £4200–£6400 per annum (Dhingra et al. 2016), with this drop in household finances and resulting economic instability hitting low-income households the hardest. The *Enduring Love?* study highlighted the stress on the couple relationship as a result of austerity-driven reductions in family finances, welfare benefits and job prospects, and contributed, thereby, to longstanding evidence about the adverse impact of stressors such as financial insecurity on couple relationships (Walker et al. 2010). Brexit can be arguably understood, then, as one of the most significant threats to relationship stability in over a generation when it is set alongside the current British government's political determination to maintain austerity measures in its long-term neo-liberal project of welfare state cuts (Taylor Gooby, 2016).

This tumultuous contemporary political arena, however, has spawned positive strategic political alliances. Echoing previous solidarity movements that emerged under Prime Minister Margaret Thatcher, groups such as Lesbians and Gays Support the Migrants (LSGM) are looking to reach out beyond their immediate boundaries. Forms of exchange and the circulation of goods are being reimagined as austerity and lack of resources require people to become evermore resourceful and recycle, barter, and look out for one another. These everyday practices of 'making do' may be a harsh reality for those struggling to pay the rent or provide food for the household, but they also have the potential to foster friendships and engender support networks that help to sustain individuals as well as couple relationships (Hall and Jayne 2016; Hall and Holmes 2017). Similar allegiances have been formed as a result of the UK's housing crisis, particularly in London where social housing tenants, private renters, architects, planners, celebrities and union members have protested together about the loss of family homes due to regeneration projects and prohibitive rents (McCabe and Duxbury, 2015).

The housing crisis remains, however, a pressing one for couple relationships because, despite the rhetoric of home and home-making that pervades UK politics (Nowicki, 2017), the importance of home for establishing and sustaining couple relationships is not acknowledged in housing policy. Many young people, for example, face major difficulties in finding a home in which to 'settle down' because of the lack of social housing, the prohibitive costs of home ownership, insecure employment and welfare cuts (Hoolachan, McKee, Moore, and Soaita, 2017). At the same time, the so-called 'bedroom tax', introduced by the Coalition Government in 2013 reduced working age, social housing tenants' eligibility for housing benefit (Gov.UK, 2017) when they were understood to have too many bedrooms (Gibb, 2015). This reduction in benefit also disregarded the need for individuals to be able to have time and space away from each other—in their *home*—something that was identified as crucial by many couples in the *Enduring Love?* study.

Relationship trends and experiences

Away from these policy and political contexts, there have been few changes in relationship and family formation trends in the UK. Cohabitation appears to be gaining momentum as a relationship choice, particularly amongst younger couples (ONS 2016), although there is every indication that cohabitation is often being chosen as a precursor to marriage or is entered into as a marriage-like relationship. It does not appear to be an expression of political distance from or ethical disavowal of marriage per se. Amongst the 'baby boomer' (65+) generation, there has been a marked increase in the number of divorcees entering into second and third marriages, more so than any other group and especially women (ONS 2017). Serial monogamy and some couples' propensity to live apart for at least the earlier period of their relationship may have increased, but there is little to suggest this has impacted on the traditional relationship ideal that is premised on sexual exclusivity and co-residence (Carter, Duncan, Stoilova and Phillips, 2015; Lampard 2017). Furthermore, and notwithstanding such shifts in relationship transitions, married or civil partner couples remain the most common family type.

It is possible to discern changes in relationship configurations, but rather than being progressive choices, these in many ways reflect wider shifts in the demographic composition of the UK population or are a response to contemporary policies. So, for example, approximately 25% of young adults aged 20 to 34 now live with their parents, an increase from 21% in 1996 (ONS 2016). Research and reports all indicate that this rise in stay-at-home youth, together with the difficulties of 'settling down' that we noted above, is a result of the lack of affordable housing and thus a lessening of choices which may have been hitherto available to their parents' generation. In our study, we heard from younger couples about the consequences on their couple relationship of living at home with parents or in shared accommodation with friends. Accounts ranged from peer support and parental relationship guidance to hiding displays of intimacy out of respect to single flatmates and to avoid the censuring eyes of overseers. This imposed constraint sometimes pushed physical affection and intimacy to the furtive corners of the household and in so doing fostered a sense of illicit excitement. In other instances, it reinforced a sense of guilt and shame, especially amongst LGBTQ couples; here, discomfort around public displays of affection (PDAs) was brought home, literally. Heteronormative frames of reference adversely shaped queer couples' public-private lives, determining which displays of affection could be displayed where and when.

Perhaps the most marked shift in relationship composition is the increase in the number of intercultural relationships in contemporary Britain. Nearly 1 in 10 people who were living as part of a couple were in an inter-ethnic relationship; this has increased from 7% in 2001 (ONS 2014). In London, the city which comprised the highest 'remain' vote in the 2016 EU referendum, more than 100,000 couples comprise a British national in a relationship with someone of another EU nationality (Independent, 2016b). For these couples being together and having a consolidated sense of 'the couple' as a relational unit requires money, time, and effort. However, international migration and transnational relationships are becoming increasingly mired in regulation, and in the context of 'austerity Britain', class-based moralism and regulation intersect with long-standing exclusionary discourses on ethnicity, national belonging and citizenship to govern and contain intimate kin connections (Sirriyeh 2015).

Micro and macro networks of relations intersect and overlap in everyday interactions, and in these emotional scenarios, people feel the immediacy of their intimate connections to each other and their significant others (Fink and Gabb, forthcoming). Here, in this book, we focus on the materiality of experience: we focus the analytical lens onto the momentary and emotionality (Gabb and Fink, 2015). This has required us to drill down into data, moving beyond description and 'the personal' to examine the ways in which public-private lives intersect. Rather than closing the door of the couple household and looking inwards, we have also accounted for the ways in which the outside (political) is manifest within everyday lives and loves. The national, European and international political contexts that frame this preface fall outside the timeframe of this book and ostensibly the explicit remit of the *Enduring Love?* study; instead there are insights into the ways in which couples endure in the face of underlying personal, cultural and socio-economic adversities. The stories of interracial couples explore how they negotiate their individual differences and in some instances how these manifest in challenges to dominant narratives of 'the couple' as a dyadic unit, embedded as they are within ideas and experiences of the extended family (see also Gabb and Singh 2014a). Such insights have already attracted significant attention from policy makers and relationship support advisors. They have helped to advance understandings of the meanings, practices and imaginings of quality and stability in long-term relationships (Chonody et al. 2016) and thus enabled practitioners to speak to the diverse experience and needs of couples.

As we also go on to show, the romantic ideal of finding 'the one' who will meet our emotional and sexual needs persists in the socio-cultural imaginary, but the lived reality of coupledom does not always fulfil this 'happy ever after' expectation. It is estimated that 20–25% of the British population are in relationships of poor quality (Reynolds et al. 2014) and 42% of marriages end in divorce (ONS 2012). Poor relationship quality has been identified as a major cause of family breakdown (Relationships Alliance 2014) with an adverse effect on adults' mental and physical health (Coleman and Glenn 2009) and children's behaviour (Garriga and Kiernan 2013). Conversely good relationship quality between partners is important for the health, life satisfaction and happiness of adults (Proulx et al. 2007; Robles et al. 2013) and their children (Amato 2001; Barrett et al. 2011; Cummings and Davies 2010). Whilst relationship longevity cannot be simply associated with relationship quality (van Acker 2015), a positive correlation has been shown to exist between relationship quality and relationship stability (Lavner and Bradbury 2010). Knowing how enduring relationships work is therefore crucial if policy, intervention, guidance and education are to be developed effectively. We have, therefore, sought to widely disseminate findings amongst a diverse range of audiences.

Research impact and the dissemination of findings

The *Enduring Love?* study that informs our analysis in this book was designed and advanced through cross-sectoral dialogue. At the project launch, Annabel Burns (then Deputy Director of Family Law and

Relationship Support Section, Department for Education) asked: 'How can we mainstream relationship education?' This provocation informed the study's impact strategy, resulting in engagement with a wide range of audiences through creative and tailor-made resources. In collaboration with colleagues and organisations, we have drawn on our findings to design and deliver a series of impactful materials and resources that engage with a diverse range of audiences, beyond the Higher Education sector. As a result, the *Enduring Love?* study has received cross-sectoral endorsement from key relationship organisations and has been praised because, as Ruth Sutherland (then Relate CEO) noted at the launch of our research findings, 'This evidence and research could really raise the national consciousness of [relationship] issues and put them firmly in the debate... this is a milestone.'

In partnership with Brook, findings have been 'translated' into freely accessible online materials for young people: https://www.brook.org.uk/your-life/category/relationships. Brook is a UK charity that works with over a quarter of a million young people every year and currently also delivers sex and relationships education (SRE) in 10% of UK schools. Lack of research evidence has been cited as one of the main reasons why teachers feel unsure about delivering SRE curriculum. Findings from our study provide such evidence, and with Brook, we have developed an e-learning teachers' pack for use in schools: https://www.brook.org.uk/our-work/relationships-enduring-love.

To enhance training and inform relationship intervention, findings from the study have also been disseminated to frontline relationship support staff through invited conference and workshop presentations. As the endorsement from relationship psychologist and agony aunt Susan Quilliam shows, this has fed into the refinement of relationship support services: '[This research] helps professionals in the field... who need to know about enduring love and pass that on to their clients.... With the *Enduring Love?* research at last... we have some answers.' In collaboration with Dr Reenee Singh and family systemic psychotherapists at the Tavistock Centre, one of the methods used in research fieldwork has now been adapted for use as part of the clinical assessment toolkit. Positive results from the clinical application of the emotion map method have been published in a leading clinical practice journal

(Gabb and Singh, 2014b). Research evidence has also been presented to government departments (Department for Education, Department for Work and Pensions, and the Treasury) and parliamentary policy making groups (Centre for Social Justice and Labour Policy Review), enabling them to refine their understandings of family and relationship support.

Finally, this book and its analysis underpin another 'sister' text, *The Secrets of Enduring Love* (Barker and Gabb, 2016) that was written explicitly for a general readership. This self-help text was serialized by *The Daily Mail* (1-5/02/2016), reaching a readership of 4 million, with a further 100 million website unique visitors. To complement a collection of audio-visual podcasts, initially produced to offer an accessible portal into the conceptual themes of the project (https://itunes.apple.com/itunes-u/enduring-love-for-ipod-iphone/id495106174), the study's findings have also been disseminated in a series of evidence-based films, titled *The Art of Relationships* (http://www.open.ac.uk/researchprojects/art-of-relationships/). These were produced in collaboration with filmmaker Steve Geliot, and were first shown at the Royal Society of Arts, London (27/05/2016) and are now hosted online (OpenLearn, YouTube, Vimeo). These films were designed as an accessible resource through which to provoke wider public reflection on personal relationship experience and to facilitate explorations of 'Art as a pathway to impact' (Langdridge et al., forthcoming). This combination of rich and wide-ranging resources has been in part prompted by the extensive media engagement which accompanied the study's findings. Broadcast features included live interviews on BBC TV News Channel, and multiple national and international radio stations. Published items featured in the *New York Post* (USA), *Le Point* (France), *The Age* (Australia), *South China Morning Post* and all major UK newspapers. A Media Impact Report on the scope and scale of this initial coverage (13/01-21/02/2014) evidenced audience reach of over 72 million people (Precise 2014). The extent of this coverage thus moved beyond dissemination of findings to scholarly audiences, prompting policy discussion and shaping wider public debate on how relationships endure.

Here, then, in *Couple Relationships in the 21st Century*, we present a detailed and vivid analysis of what couples ordinarily do to sustain partnerships day by day and over life course, written for researchers, relationship support organisations, psychologists, counsellors and an informed general public. The book brings together our findings in a cohesive and readily accessible format that will resonate with all those interested in researching or working with couple and family relationships. The cultural fascination with relationships and a long-standing political concern about the effects of relationship breakdown on family life and society more broadly is addressed through this timely intervention, adding a critical edge that draws on rigorously generated research evidence. Across the chapters, we engage with and unsettle media, political and policy interest in couple relationships and also address some of the absences in academic knowledge about couples in long-term relationships and the interiority of their personal lives. In so doing, we aim to invigorate understandings of the state of relationships in contemporary Britain and highlight the ways in which conceptualizations of 'the couple' and coupledom intersect with and challenge pervasive cultural ideals of finding 'the one' and living 'happily ever after'. The result of this critical engagement is a book that significantly extends knowledge of personal and family lives and provides crucial research evidence for the development of effective policy making, couple and family support, and relationship education materials.

Jacqui Gabb and Janet Fink

References

Amato, P., & Booth, A. (2001). The Legacy of Parents' Marital Discord: Consequences for Children's Marital Quality. *Journal of Personality and Social Psychology, 81*(4), 627–638.

Barker, M. J., & Gabb, J. (2016). *The Secrets of Enduring Love.* London: Vermillion Random House.

Barrett, H., Chang, Y-S. & Walker, J. (2011). *Improving Children's Outcomes by Supporting Couple Relationships, Reducing Family Conflict and Addressing Domestic Violence.* London: Centre for Excellence and Outcomes in Children and Young People's Services.

Carter, J., Duncan, S., Stoilova, M., & Phillips, M. (2105). Sex, Love and Security: Accounts of Distance and Commitment in Living Apart Together Relationships. *Sociology, 50*(3): 576–593.

Clarke, J., & Newman, J. (2017). "People in This Country have Had Enough of Experts": Brexit and the Paradoxes of Populism. *Critical Policy Studies, 11*(1), 101–116.

Chonody, J., Gabb, J., Killian, M., & Dunk-West, P. (2016). Measuring Relationship Quality in an International Study: Exploratory and Confirmatory Factor Validity. *Research on Social Work Practice*: doi: 10.1177/1049731516631120.

Coleman, L., & Glenn, F. (2009). *When Couples Part*. London: OnePlusOne Publications.

Cummings, E. M., & Davies, P.T. (2010). *Marital Conflict and Children: An Emotional Security Perspective*. New York: The Guilford Press.

Currie, S. (2016). Reflecting on Brexit: Migration Myths and What Comes Next for EU Migrants in the UK? *Journal of Social Welfare and Family Law, 38*(3), 337–342.

Dhingra, S., Ottaviano, G., Sampson, T., & Van Reenen, J. (2016). The Consequences of Brexit for UK Trade and Living Standards. CEP Brexit Analysis No. 2 http://cep.lse.ac.uk/pubs/download/brexit02.pdf

Fink, J., & Gabb, J. (forthcoming). To Have and To Hold? The Relationality of Emotions and Couples' Relationships in 21st Century Britain. In k. Barclay, J. Meek, & A. Thomson (Eds.), *Courtship, Marriage, and Marriage Breakdown: Perspectives from the History of Emotions*. London: Routledge.

Gabb, J., & Fink, J. (2015). Telling Moments: Qualitative Mixed Methods Research on Personal Relationships and Family Lives. *Sociology, 49*(5), 970–987.

Gabb, J., & Singh, R. (2014a). Reflections on the Challenges of Understanding Racial, Cultural and Sexual Differences in Couple Relationship Research. *Journal of Family Therapy, 37*(2), 210–227.

Gabb, J., & Singh, R. (2014b). The Uses of Emotion Maps in Research and Clinical Practice with Families and Couples: Methodological Innovation and Critical Inquiry. *Family Process, 54*(1), 185–197.

Garriga, A., & Kiernan, K. (2013). Parents' Relationship Quality, Mother-child Relations and Children's Behaviour Problems: Evidence from the UK Millennium Cohort Study. Working Paper. Retrieved 6 Feb 2015 from http://www.york.ac.uk/media/spsw/documents/research-andpublications/Garriga-and-Kiernan-WP2013.pdf

Gibb, K. (2015). The Multiple Policy Failures of the UK Bedroom Tax. *International Journal of Housing Policy, 15*(2), 148–166.

Gov.UK. (2016). Become a British Citizen. https://www.gov.uk/becoming-a-british-citizen/check-if-you-can-apply

Gov.UK. (2017) Housing Benefit. https://www.gov.uk/housing-benefit/what-youll-get

Guardian. (2017). UK Denies Residency to London-Born Children of Dutch-Spanish Couple. https://www.theguardian.com/politics/2017/apr/13/european-couple-stunned-as-uk-born-children-denied-residency

Guardian. (2016a). Huge Backlog as EU Citizens Rush to Secure British Residency. https://www.theguardian.com/uk-news/2016/nov/30/eu-citizens-in-uk-home-office-residency-applications-right-to-remain-before-brexit-talks

Guardian. (2016b). Law Fails Poorer Families Going Through Relationship Breakdown. https://www.theguardian.com/lifeandstyle/2016/nov/09/legal-aid-cuts-no-fault-divorce

Hall, S. M., & Holmes, H. (2017, May). Making Do and Getting by? Beyond a Romantic Politics of Austerity and Crisis. *Discover Society*. www.discover society.org

Hall, S. M., & Jayne, M. (2016). Make, Mend and Befriend: Geographies of Austerity, Crafting and Friendship in Contemporary Cultures of Dressmaking. *Gender, Place & Culture, 23*(2), 216–234.

Hobolt, S. B. (2016). The Brexit Vote: A Divided Nation, a Divided Continent. *Journal of European Public Policy, 23*(9), 1259–1277.

Hoolachan, J., McKee, K., Moore, T., & Soaita, A. M. (2017). "Generation Rent" and the Ability to "Settle Down": Economic and Geographical Variation in Young People's Housing Transitions. *Journal of Youth Studies, 20*(1), 63–78.

Independent. (2016a). Brexit Arguments Causing Rifts Between Couples. http://www.independent.co.uk/news/uk/home-news/brexit-anxieties-issue-troubled-couples-relationship-counsellors-experts-a7500876.html

Independent. (2016b). How Breaking Up the EU Could Break Up Couples. http://www.independent.co.uk/news/uk/politics/how-breaking-up-the-eu-could-break-up-couples-a7000156.html

Jessop, B. (2017). The Organic Crisis of the British State: Putting Brexit in its Place. *Globalizations, 14*(1), 133–141.

Lampard, R. (2016). Living Together in a Sexually Exclusive Relationship: An Enduring, Pervasive Ideal? *Families, Relationships and Societies, 5*(1), 23–41.

Langdridge, D., Gabb, J., & Lawson, J. (forthcoming). Art as a Pathway to Impact: An "Affective" Evaluation.

Lavner, J., & Bradbury, T. (2010). Patterns of Change in Marital Satisfaction over the Newlywed Years. *Journal of Marriage and Family, 72*(5), 1171–1187.

McCabe, J., & Duxbury, N. (2015). Rise of the Housing Activist. *Inside Housing*, May 1. http://www.insidehousing.co.uk/analysis-and-data/investigations/rise-of-the-housing-activist/7009545.article

Nowicki, M. (2017). A Britain That Everyone is Proud to Call Home? The Bedroom Tax, Political Rhetoric and Home Unmaking in UK Housing Policy. *Social and Cultural Geography*. http://www.tandfonline.com/doi/full/10.1080/14649365.2017.1296179

ONS. (2014). Census Analysis: What Does the 2011 Census Tell Us About Inter-Ethnic Relationships? https://www.ons.gov.uk/peoplepopulationand community/birthsdeathsandmarriages/marriagecohabitationandcivil partnerships/articles/whatdoesthe2011censustellusaboutinterethnic relationships/2014-07-03

ONS. (2016). Families and Households in the UK. https://www.ons.gov. uk/peoplepopulationandcommunity/birthsdeathsandmarriages/families/ bulletins/familiesandhouseholds/2016

ONS. (2017). Marriages in England and Wales. https://www.ons.gov.uk/peo- plepopulationandcommunity/birthsdeathsandmarriages/marriagecohabita- tionandcivilpartnerships/bulletins/marriagesinenglandandwalesprovisional/2 014#at-what-age-are-couples-getting-married

Precise. (2014). *The Open University Enduring Love? Media Impact Report*. London: Precise.

Proulx, C., Helms, H., & Buehler, C. (2007). Marital Quality and Personal Well-being: A Meta-analysis. *Journal of Marriage and Family, 69*(3), 576–593.

Relationships Alliance. (2014). The Relationships Manifesto: Strengthening Relationships. Retrieved on 29 October 2014, from http://www.relate.org. uk/files/relate/ramanifestoprint.pdf

Reynolds J., Houlston, C., & Coleman, L. (2014). Understanding Relationship Quality. OnePlusOne.

Robles R., Slatcher, R., Tombello, J., & McGinn, M. (2014). Marital Quality and Health: A Meta-analytic Review. *Psychological Bulletin, 140*(1), 140–148.

Singh R., & Dada, M. (2017). Intercultural Couples in a Divided World. *Discover Society* www.discoversociety.org

Sirriyeh, A. (2015). 'All You Need Is Love and £18,600': Class and the UK's New Family Migration Rules'. *Critical Social Policy, 35*(2), 228–247.

Taylor Gooby, P. (2016). The Divisive Welfare State. *Social Policy and Administration, 50*(6), 712–733.

van Acker, L. (2015). Investing in Couple Relationship Education in the UK: A Gender Perspective. *Social Policy & Society, 14*(1), 1–14.

Walker, J., Barrett, H., Wilson, G., & Chang, Y-S. (2010). *Understanding the Needs of Adults (particularly parents) Regarding Relationship Support*. Research Brief DCSF-RBX-10-01. London: DCFS.

Series Editors' Preface

The remit of the *Palgrave Macmillan Studies in Family and Intimate Life* series is to publish major texts, monographs and edited collections focusing broadly on the sociological exploration of intimate relationships and family organisation. As editors, we think such a series is timely. Expectations, commitments and practices have changed significantly in intimate relationship and family life in recent decades. This is very apparent in patterns of family formation and dissolution, demonstrated by trends in cohabitation, marriage and divorce. Changes in household living patterns over the last 20 years have also been marked, with more people living alone, adult children living longer in the parental home and more 'non-family' households being formed. Furthermore, there have been important shifts in the ways people construct intimate relationships. There are few comfortable certainties about the best ways of being a family man or woman, with once conventional gender roles no longer being widely accepted. The normative connection between sexual relationships and marriage or marriage-like relationships is also less powerful than it once was. Not only is greater sexual experimentation accepted, but it is now accepted at an earlier age. Moreover heterosexuality is no longer the only mode of sexual relationship given legitimacy. In Britain as elsewhere, gay and lesbian partnerships are now socially and legally endorsed to a degree hardly imaginable in the mid-twentieth century. Increases in lone-parent families, the rapid growth of different types of stepfamily, the de-stigmatization of births outside marriage and the rise in couples 'living apart together' all provide further examples of the ways that 'being a couple', 'being a parent' and 'being a family' have diversified in recent years.

The fact that change in family life and intimate relationships has been so pervasive has resulted in renewed research interest from sociologists and other scholars. Increasing amounts of public funding have been directed to family research in recent years, in terms of both individual projects and the creation of family research centres of different hues. This research activity has been accompanied by the publication of some very important and influential books exploring different aspects of shifting family experience, in Britain and elsewhere. The *Palgrave Macmillan Studies in Family and Intimate Life* series hopes to add to this list of influential research-based texts, thereby contributing to existing knowledge and informing current debates. Our main audience consists of academics and advanced students, though we intend that the books in the series will be accessible to a more general readership who wish to understand better the changing nature of contemporary family life and personal relationships.

We see the remit of the series as wide. The concept of 'family and intimate life' will be interpreted in a broad fashion. While the focus of the series will clearly be sociological, we take family and intimacy as being inclusive rather than exclusive. The series will cover a range of topics concerned with family practices and experiences, including, for example, partnership, marriage, parenting, domestic arrangements, kinship, demographic change, intergenerational ties, life course transitions, step-families, gay and lesbian relationships, lone-parent households, and also non-familial intimate relationships such as friendships. We also wish to foster comparative research, as well as research on under-studied populations. The series will include different forms of book. Most will be theoretical or empirical monographs on particular substantive topics, though some may also have a strong methodological focus. In addition, we see edited collections as also falling within the series' remit, as well as translations of significant publications in other languages. Finally we intend that the series has an international appeal, in terms of both topics covered and authorship. Our goal is for the series to provide a forum for family sociologists conducting research in various societies, and not solely in Britain.

—*Graham Allan, Lynn Jamieson and*
David Morgan

Acknowledgements

We would like to thank the Economic and Social Research Council for funding *The Enduring Love? Couple Relationships in the 21st Century* study (RES-062-23-3056) on which this book is based. The study was initially conceived as part of a wider thematic area that was convened through the Intimate Futures and Relational Lives (IFRL) Research Group and generously supported by The Open University (OU). The IFRL initiative enabled us to bring together those working in professional practice, the public sector and the media to explore how research in this field might address existing questions and concerns and explore emerging issues. This meeting proved crucial in establishing the funded study's dialogic approach and ensuring the success of its public engagement and impact activities. Thanks are particularly due, here, to Susanna Abse (CEO, Tavistock Centre for Couple Relationships); Penny Mansfield, CBE (Director, OnePlusOne); Ruth Sutherland (CEO, Relate); Nick Turner (Relate); and Janet Walker, OBE (Relate/University of Newcastle).

We would also like to thank the team of researchers who worked with us on the study. Martina Klett-Davies played an invaluable role as research associate, and Danielle Pearson, Tam Sanger and Reenee Singh made significant contributions to ensuring the success of the study's fieldwork. The knowledge and experience of Meg Barker and Susan Quilliam were crucial to the development of the study's media strategy. We are also grateful to Laura Harvey and Mark Carrigan who were consistently helpful colleagues. More generally, the Faculty of Social Sciences at The Open University supported the research in many different ways, and we thank the many staff whose expertise, advice and insights we drew on, often remorselessly, over the years in which we were managing the research. The Open University students and alumni were eager and attentive audiences at presentations of our findings at OU-hosted conferences, seminars and workshops and so made these events all the more enjoyable.

We have spoken about the study and our findings at countless venues, and we are grateful for the generous and productive feedback from academic and policy/practitioner colleagues alike. All have contributed to the development of our ideas, provoked us to ask more or different questions of our data, or encouraged us to think about collaborations for future research projects.

Finally, and most importantly, thanks are due to the couples who took part in this study. They were generous with their time and hospitality over the weeks in which the fieldwork was conducted and were remaining committed to their involvement in the research and to what we were aiming to achieve. This book is dedicated to them.

Contents

List of Figures

List of Tables

1

Introduction

Researching couple relationships

In her book *Ordinary Affects*, Kathleen Stewart (2007) endeavours to slow down the pace of analytical thinking as a means of speaking to, and taking account of, complex and uncertain objects in order 'to fashion some form of address that is adequate to their form; to find something to say about ordinary affects by performing some of the intensity and texture that makes them habitable and animate' (2007, p. 4). In this book, we maintain there are no more 'complex or uncertain objects' than long-term couple relationships, and that a similar epistemological strategy is needed to examine how couple relationships *endure* and in what ways they are *endured*. By concentrating attention on the 'ordinary affects' which combine to create the texture of couple relationships, and through which the tensile strength of couple relationships is constituted, the book explores how relationships are sustained in the moment and over time. Moreover, in attending to the minutiae and mundanities of everyday feelings, acts and gestures that often go unseen in enduring relationships, we also bring into view the 'intensity and texture' of those elements that connect two people and shape their intimate lives together.

© The Author(s) 2018
J. Gabb, J. Fink, *Couple Relationships in the 21st Century*, Palgrave Macmillan Studies in Family and Intimate Life, DOI 10.1007/978-3-319-59698-3_1

Our aims in this endeavour and in the book more broadly are twofold. The first is to extend understandings of couple relationships by turning the analytic lens onto the many heterosexual and non-heterosexual (lesbian, gay, bisexual and queer – LGBQ) couples who remain together for significant periods of time, thereby shifting attention away from serial or transitory relationships (Montemurro, 2014) and relationship breakdown (Coleman & Glenn, 2010), which have largely dominated much of the research in this field. Our analysis draws from the *Enduring Love?* study[1] which examined long-term couple relationships. Such couples have received little sustained academic attention in recent years and their inclusion in socio-cultural, policy and political debates about relationships and family life has tended to be as romanticised or aspirational relationship formations. By addressing these lacunae in research and resisting idealised and often deeply 'traditional' views on the meanings of stability and quality in relationships, we thus seek to portray a more complex and nuanced account of how couples live and love in contemporary Britain. In so doing we illustrate the intersections of structure and agency, past and present, realities and dreams, and culture and context.

Our second aim is to extend a *practices approach* to the study of couple relationships in order to focus attention on couples' experiences and feelings, especially where these are situated and materialised in the home. Despite the extensive use of 'family practices' and 'practices of intimacy' in studies of families and personal lives, a practices approach is curiously absent in research concerned with couple relationships – as we go on to discuss. This has left a particular gap in knowledge about what couples *do*, together and together apart, in the privacy of their homes. For those in abusive relationships, home can be a place of insecurity, distress and fear but for the couples in our study, who viewed their lives together in largely positive terms, home signified permanence and commitment. We thus suggest that attending to the spatial dimension of couple practices brings into view how ideas and experiences of home are crucial in building a sense of togetherness and creating opportunities to nurture relationships (Neustatter, 2012). We hope, therefore, that the book's analysis of the importance of home as a point of actual and imagined stability amidst the fluid and complex emotional dynamics of couple relationships will be of relevance to professionals and practitioners working to implement effective relationship education and support services. We also hope that our emphasis on the home as occupying a special place in couples' imaginary of long-term relationships will provoke further policy debate about the effects on couples working to sustain their relationships of, not least, housing benefit changes, the 'bedroom tax', homelessness and the shortage of affordable homes in Britain.

Demographic and policy contexts

In England and Wales, 42 per cent of marriages end in divorce (Office for National Statistics (ONS), 2012) with between 200,000 and 250,000 couples separating every year (Coleman & Glenn, 2009). Recent trends in the divorce rate indicate a decline (ONS, 2012) but nevertheless the number of divorces in England and Wales remains high. There has also been a corollary long-term decline in the marriage rate since the early 1970s. In response to this climate of make-and-break relationships, much recent policy, academic and professional research has been concerned with the causes and effects of relationship dissolution. Studies have tended to focus on the 'stressors' that contribute to relationship breakdown (Walker, Barrett, Wilson, & Chang, 2010) and the adverse impact of 'marital distress' and 'family fragmentation' on the health and well-being of men, women and children (Markham & Halford, 2005). At the same time, other studies have suggested that 85 per cent of people have a good relationship with their partner (Sherwood, Kneale, & Bloomfield, 2014), while the married couple with or without children remains the most common type of relationship unit in the United Kingdom (Beaumont, 2011). Seven in ten households are still headed by married couples and figures show an increase in marriages of 5.3 per cent between 2011 and 2012 (equating to one marriage every two minutes), with the largest percentage of 21 per cent and 25 per cent, respectively, among women and men aged between 65 and 69 (ONS, 2014). In the first five years of civil partnerships (December 2005–2010), over 46,000 same-sex partnerships had been registered (ONS, 2011), pointing to the enduring appeal of couple relationships across the sexual spectrum.

Political and policy interest in this area has tended to concentrate on families with children, and particularly their parenting practices, rather than couple relationships per se. From New Labour government (1997–2010) initiatives such as *Every Child Matters* (DfES, 2003), *Every Parent Matters* (DfCSF, 2007) and *Support for All: Families and Relationships* (DfCSF, 2010) through to Conservative-Liberal Democratic coalition government (2010–2015) reforms, including the Children and Families Act (2014) and the *Troubled Families* programme, there has been little discernible shift in policy orientation. The rhetoric of 'hard-working families' and the importance of quality relationships for family life remain recurrent themes. These have, however, increasingly served to cleave apart those who are understood to be striving to help themselves and those whose lives have been constituted through discourses of blame around welfare dependency, failed relationships and 'poor' parenting (Fink & Lomax, 2014). This latter group have then, in turn, become subject to 'a whole raft of bruising austerity measures' introduced by the coalition government (O'Hara, 2014, p. 1). In these policy and political contexts, love is often perceived as both the solution and the problem (Wilkinson, 2013). Love can sustain couple and family relationships in the face of adversities; its absence destines relationships to fail, financial hardship to ensue and greater welfare support to be needed. The concerted government focus on family breakdown (Centre for Social Justice (CSJ), 2014b) and its associated policy directives such as the introduction of a transferable tax allowance for married couples (CSJ, 2013) are thus positioned as a necessary response to the 'social damage' caused by separation and the annual cost of family breakdown, estimated at £44 billion (CSJ, 2014a).

Such narrow policy responses have not, however, been without their critics. The Relationships Alliance, formed of four leading relationship support organisations – Relate, Marriage Care, OnePlusOne and the Tavistock Centre for Couple Relationships – has, for example, suggested a range of alternative policy proposals to support couple relationships that go beyond the purely financial (Relationships Alliance, 2013; Relationships Alliance, 2014). One of its recommendations is the targeted provision of services at those life transition points, such as unemployment, becoming a parent and retiring, that have long been recognised in academic, policy and practitioner research as 'stressors' (Walker et al., 2010) that some couples struggle to cope with. At a 'Relationship Summit' (College of General Practitioners, London, 18 August 2014), in the long run-up to the 2015 general election, Prime Minister David Cameron announced that all future domestic policies would have to pass a 'family test' that would examine their impact on family relationships. This book, then, like the rationale behind the Relationships Alliance's recommendations and manifesto, speaks to the importance of attending to the intersections of everyday emotions and experiences in couple relationships when seeking to understand how people manage the challenges and difficulties that can be encountered in long-term relationships.

Academic contexts

Different academic disciplines have taken different methodological approaches to the study of couple relationships in order to interrogate a range of issues and concerns. Work completed under the umbrella of social psychology has, for example, emphasised how people perceive their couple relationships as continually developing and lasting ventures (Duck, 2007; Mashek & Aron, 2004) – a finding reinforced by the *Enduring Love?* study wherein couples regularly imagined their futures together. Research from longitudinal studies of cohorts (born in 1946, 1958 and 1970) provides a generational dimension, highlighting coterminous continuities as well as change such as strikingly high levels of relationship dissatisfaction among the younger age cohort. Gender remains significant across the cohorts, driving changes in couple relationships, notably as a result of women's increased participation in the labour market and education. Moreover, women in couple relationships seem to be expressing more ambivalence about whether children are 'an important part of life' (Ferri & Smith, 2003, p. 124), although they feel less positively about childlessness than men (Koropeckyj-Cox & Pendell, 2007). Here, as our findings also illustrate, the intersections of gender and parenthood are crucial. Many childless couples believe that they have a closer relationship than parental couples (Hird & Abshoff, 2000). Comparative work with childfree couples and new parents in the early stages of parenthood supports this assertion (Lawrence, Rothman, Cobb, Rothman, & Bradbury,

2008), although research on how intimacy might change or even increase during childrearing years is limited (Kouneski & Olson, 2004).

Sociologically informed UK research *purely* focused on understanding the couple relationship was, until recently, quite dated (Askham, 1984; Bell & Newby, 1976; Blood & Wolfe, 1960; Clark, 1991; Edgell, 1980; Fitzpatrick, 1988). The contemporary relevance of these studies of marriage and long-term couple relationships does, however, remain (Lewis, 2001; Mansfield & Collard, 1988; Marsden, 1990) and has enabled us to interrogate the extent to which professed transformations in intimacy (Giddens, 1992) have impacted on lived experience. For example, it is claimed that there has been a wholesale democratisation of intimacy which has brought about a sea change in personal and sexual commitments (Beck & Beck-Gersheim, 1995), reconfiguring intimate life (Giddens, 1992; Jamieson, 1998). Attention has thus been drawn to the diversity of intimate practices and family arrangements (Jamieson, Morgan, Crow, & Allan, 2006; Williams, 2004) and relationship–residence formations (Duncan & Phillips, 2008; Roseneil & Budgeon, 2004) that can be found in contemporary Britain, particularly around heterosexual (Hockey, Meah, & Robinson, 2010; Hooff, 2013) and same-sex (Heaphy, Smart, & Einarsdottir, 2013) partnerships. Notwithstanding such diversity, the *romantic ideal* of one partner meeting all our emotional and sexual needs does appear to remain steadfast, stretching across differences in sexuality and circumstance (Smart, 2007). Furthermore, while the democratisation of love (Giddens, 1992) may be enshrouded in the rhetoric of egalitarianism, the feminist critique of this social theorising draws on a wealth of compelling empirical research evidence to highlight a quite different reality (Jamieson, 1999). The feminist adage that 'it starts when you sink into his arms and ends with your arms in his sink' still often rings true *in practice*, as we discuss later in the book.

Socio-cultural contexts

The continuing investment in the idea of 'the couple' saturates the cultural imaginary and is reinforced by a burgeoning mass-culture industry which 'tickles our senses with an abundance of images, fragrances, tastes and music' (Lindqvist, 1996, p. 47) related to ideas of romance, love and eroticism. Couple relationships appear repeatedly as a topic of popular and journalistic interest (Blyth, 2010; Figes, 2010; Gottlieb, 2010; Reibstein, 2006), historical research (Langhamer, 2013; Waller, 2010), autobiographical and biographical studies (Fraser, 2010; Hodgkins, 2012), TV documentaries (BBC4, 2012) and in Hollywood blockbusters and European art-house cinema. Flurries of media reporting appear in response to statistics about marriage and divorce, including emerging relationship phenomena such as 'grey divorce' (ONS, 2012), and extensive features are written around new research such as that reporting seeming changes in sexual behaviour and attitudes (National Survey of Sexual Attitudes and Lifestyles (Natsal), 2013). Couples celebrating golden and diamond wedding anniversaries are regularly featured in local press and asked for 'personal tips' on maintaining relationships, while the proliferation of chat shows and 'real life' magazines, which take as their focus the intimate disclosure of personal emotions around countless relationship issues, adds weight to the argument that we are living in a therapeutic culture (Furedi, 2004).

Running alongside the insistent presence of couple relationships in these different print, online and visual sources is an equally sustained focus on couples in popular therapy, evidenced through the attention afforded to couple relationships in self-help books, therapeutic TV programmes and advice columns in newspapers, magazines and online. As Eldén has argued:

> Therapists, life coaches, and other experts are eager to share their analysis of what is wrong in people's lives and to offer methods, tools and solutions to achieve a happy life. (Eldén, 2011, p. 144)

Achieving a 'happy life' in the context of our study is understood to require *work* in order for the relationship to 'succeed'. Indeed, such has been the influence of this popular therapeutic discourse that the sociocultural and political contexts in which couple relationships are situated and imagined have increasingly drawn on the language of working at relationships, relationships that work and supporting couples to make relationships work better. This 'working at it agenda' also features consistently in professionally oriented guidance and practice directed at family support, intervention and relationship advice (Chang & Barrett, 2009).

We do not have the scope to engage with the vast volume of literature in this ever-growing self-help market (for a critical review see Barker, Gill, & Harvey, 2015). There is, however, much to commend in a lot of this literature. Indeed, our findings on relationship work echo the qualities and strategies recommended in some of its key texts. For example, in *The Five Love Languages* (2010), author and psychologist Gary Chapman identifies five essential ingredients in a successful couple relationship: words of affirmation; quality time; receiving gifts; acts of service; and physical touch. While the sociological critique of 'emotion culture' and the professed reflexive turn has quite rightly pointed to the power of silence and the significance of what we do not talk about (Brownlie, 2014), our findings can add to the therapeutic field. Our robust, large-scale research evidence is attentive to both what is said and what is left unspoken – and, importantly, what is communicated when words are not spoken. Actions (or, in our terms, practices) can, we would argue, speak louder than words. Moreover, the critical lens that we use to analyse our data draws on and extends a range of theorising to interrogate and understand the richness of multidimensional experience in lived and living long-term couple relationships.

Couple practices

Relationships, as we have noted, are always situated at the intersections of different political, policy and socio-cultural contexts. They are also experienced through everyday, often mundane interactions, gestures and practices. Our analysis is, therefore, informed by the significance of context and underpinned by the conceptual framework of 'relating practices' (Gabb, 2011), particularly the ways in which this can be used to critically engage with ideas and experiences of the couple and coupledom. We develop this framework in two ways. First, as a means to examine what couples ordinarily do and through which patterns of relating can be traced. Second, as an opportunity to engage with and extend the *practices approach*, which has been so influential in British family sociology and curiously absent in extant couple research. There are a few notable exceptions to this absence including work on 'narratives of couple practice' in the context of lesbian and gay ageing (Heaphy, 2009); how couple practices reinforce the heterosexual unequal division of household labour (Robinson, 2003); and the impact of faith on couples' conflict management (Butler, Gardner, & Bird, 1998). Even in these instances, however, the term is only fleetingly used and not deployed as an analytical tool.

In contemporary studies of families, intimacy and personal life, there has been a shift away from structure and social units of analysis onto the ways in which relationships become materialised and experienced through everyday practices. The concept 'family practices' (Morgan, 1996, 2011) draws attention to the processes by which families are made and remade through interactions and routines, serving to dispel earlier functionalist reasoning that analysed 'the family' as a unitary object. Family practices focuses attention onto relational connections and the multifarious ways that families are created through sets of caring and intimate relationships (Gabb, 2008): families are what families do (Silva & Smart, 1999). A practices approach, as Morgan (2011) notes, embraces both individual and relational behaviour, and habituated routines that may reproduce and sustain pre-existing ways of being together. Practices, in this context, are already partially shaped by 'legal prescriptions, economic constraints and cultural conditions' (Morgan, 2011, p. 7), but this does not irrevocably debar variation. Instead, it facilitates interrogation of differences and diversity in experience *across* and *within* households (Jamieson, 2005).

Extending out of this approach, studies of personal life have focused their analysis on everyday 'practices of intimacy'. Practices of intimacy refer to the things that people do to 'enable, generate and sustain a subjective sense of closeness and being attuned and special to each other' (Jamieson, 2011, p. 1). In this vein, work on intimate citizenship has usefully situated interpersonal relationships as reflexive sites of agency that are shaped by, and in turn shape, public institutions (Plummer, 2003). Reflexivity in this context does not mean an open book through which couples can freely create themselves and their relationship. Cultural scripts remain crucial in how people develop couple and sexual relationships and perceive themselves as intimates (Duncombe & Marsden, 1995; Jackson & Scott, 2004). Nevertheless, like its conceptual companion family practices, practices of intimacy shift the research agenda away from a functionalist imperative that reifies different forms of relationships into categorical types. It draws attention to the qualitative dimensions of interpersonal intimacies and, in so doing, reflects wider social changes in the affective patterning of relationships, wherein marriage, divorce and remarriage are commonplace (Gabb, 2008). It is important to note here, too, that this focus on practices is not just of academic interest. It enables us see why some contexts may be able to support some kinds of practices more than others and 'help us to think through what the consequences might be for individuals and the wider social fabric when such support is modified' (Jamieson, 2011, p. 4).

The closest conceptual relative of intimacy is love and, as such, it is not surprising that research on practices of intimacy also draws on the rich vein of work that interrogates love (Bawin-Legros, 2004). As Lynn Jamieson (2011) says, relationships that are perceived and mutually experienced as relationships of love typically involve practices of intimacy; conversely, expressions of love as a feeling is a practice of intimacy and a practice that can build intimacy. Being in love may *feel* like a heartfelt emotion that knows no bounds and overwhelms all reason, but alongside the cultural repertoires of intimacy, love is also scripted. Who and how we love is shaped by our cultural contexts (Stacey, 2011) and our biographical anchors (Heaphy et al., 2013). Work loosely collected together under the sociology of emotions has shown how heteronormative conventions continue to shape understandings and the experience of love, sex and desire (Berlant, 2012; Hockey et al., 2010; Illouz, 2012; Johnson, 1996; Stacey, 2011). Cultural tropes inform how we experience such sensations as 'falling in love' (Jackson, 1993) and make sense of the most intimate of encounters, such as orgasm (Jackson & Scott, 2007). Feelings of love and practices of intimacy are thus always closely entangled in the socio-cultural and political contexts in which love is discursively defined and given meaning (Smart, 2007).

Our analytical approach to interrogating the meanings and practices of couple relationships also builds on and problematises the concerted queer critique that has been rallied against 'the couple' and coupledom. This critique has demonstrated how 'the nuclear family and conjugal couple-dom are being invoked in political discourses as the bedrock of post-war

Britain' (Wilkinson, 2013, p. 206), with the equality rights agenda further extending 'the couple' ideology through same-sex partnerships (Peel & Harding, 2008). Here, the couple is characterised as the epitome of a neo-liberalist agenda, wherein power is divested to the individual as part of wider socio-cultural transformations of intimacy (Giddens, 1992), while corresponding regulatory regimes such as welfare and social policies close down other intimate opportunities (Smith, 2007) and instantiate compulsory coupledom (Wilkinson, 2013). Through such seemingly progressive equal rights developments, it has been argued that a reactionary 'mononormativity' has been advanced (Wilkinson, 2013) serving to impose the ideology of couple culture (Budgeon, 2008).

Findings from the *Enduring Love?* study suggest an overwhelming diversity among couples and thus problematise both heteronormative understandings of 'the couple' and its queer, neo-liberal chimera. Relationships are constituted, experienced and afforded meaning through everyday experiences which make and remake couple intimacies in dynamic configurations. This provokes further reflection on the couple relationship and its slippage into, and conflation with, cultural understandings of the western heteronormative 'couple norm'. How might, for example, opening up perceived boundaries and binaries around coupledom and the couple norm make available a space to develop more nuanced appreciations of what constitutes a 'working' couple relationship? How can we understand the diversity of lived and living relationships and the possibilities for their materialisation in contemporary Britain?

Our conceptual endeavour in attending to these questions is to keep the constitutive and iterative process of *doing* relationships at the forefront of the analytical lens (Morgan, 1996), while calling attention to the 'interdependent elements that last beyond specific moments of enactment' (Phoenix & Brannen, 2013, p. 13). There are, after all, always boundaries to the practices that can be enacted and displayed – as we explore further in Chapter 5. This endeavour also acknowledges the extent to which everyday life informs the conduct and conceptualisation of much family research and study of intimate life (Gabb, 2008). Experience is embodied and located in the specificity of place (Pink, 2012); everyday practices are configured and reconfigured over time (Shove, Pantzar, & Watson, 2012). Relationships involve investments that weave together a shared past, the present day and an imagined future, which in turn illustrate a diachronic dimension to the everyday. In the following chapters we thus demonstrate how the analytical lens of couple practices can be used to unpick understandings of intimate life and the ways that couples live and love together, over time.

The book

In this introduction, we have mapped out the book's contextual and conceptual terrain and argued that a practices approach to the study of couples' lives together is crucial if we are to fully understand how long-term relationships are experienced, given meaning and sustained. To examine the constantly evolving configurations of these relationships, however, a multiple methods research design that can generate richly textured data on different dimensions of phenomena is required (Gabb, 2008). This layering approach has been variously described as pieces of a jigsaw (Gabb, 2009) or fragments of data which produce meaning through 'each twist of the analytical kaleidoscope' (McCarthy, Gillies, & Holland, 2003, p. 19). While Mason (2011, p. 80) has argued that facets (data from different methods) cast and refract light to afford 'flashes of insight' on a phenomenon (the multi-faceted gemstone), for us, there is no single gemstone. Relationships are highly complex phenomena in that the object of study is often hard to grasp, not least because it includes the individual, the couple and the social unit, as well as the biographical, socio-cultural and policy contexts in which they are embedded. The analytical foci can be difficult to sustain and, by default, are constantly evolving.

Our study used, therefore, different methods to bring into sharp relief the range of everyday practices that, when combined, build up dynamic and multidimensional understandings of the couple relationship. Diaries generated temporal data on daily routines and the moments that comprise relationship life. Emotions maps located everyday experience in the home and depicted the emotional dynamic of couple relationships. Biographical interviews focused on how relationships work, exploring relational experience across the life course. Couple collage interviews examined the socio-cultural contexts of relationships and addressed key research themes. A quantitative survey generated statistical information on relationship qualities, relationship with partner and relationship maintenance.[2] Combining data from these different methods does not, however, weave a seamless picture. As we illustrate in the following chapters, the subtle interplay of cross-cutting methodological threads enables us to retain the 'messiness' (Daly, 2003) and complexity of lives lived in and through the everyday.

The study was also informed by psycho-social approaches, which proved crucial in making sense of the research relationship and our interpretations of the data. These approaches are designed to examine intersections between the psychic and the social, locating these in the cultural context and biography of the individual (Roseneil, 2006). Researcher subjectivity is understood to be a valuable aspect of the research process (Ramazanoglu & Holland, 2002) which, we would argue, is particularly salient in studies of personal lives, where connections and mirrored reflections, ambivalence and antipathy are inevitable. We thus remained attentive to feelings that were brought up in fieldwork and analysis. Researcher field notes and pen portraits rested alongside, and informed, our readings of all data generated, *situating* the individual and couple in their relationship and biographical contexts. However, researchers' feelings and personal responses are not represented in our analysis, on the page, although we acknowledge that researcher subjectivity informs how an account is produced and analysed. We remain open, therefore, to the possibility of different interpretations of the same material since readings are not all *in the text*, but are produced out of 'a complex interaction between reader and text' (Walkerdine, 1998, p. 73).

At the same time, we are committed to advancing a sociologically informed analysis that accounts for couple relationships as a phenomenon and, as such, while we are mindful of situation, feelings and context, we examine the data thematically within and across the book. This moves beyond the case study approach that is typically associated with psycho-social studies. The study's survey data were used to scope patterns in relationship behaviour, serving to inform our analysis of the qualitative data. Qualitative data then focused the analytical lens onto emotional life and everyday relationship practices, drawing on a broad spectrum of research senses, encouraging opportunities to listen and hear, and to look and see (Back, 2007; Fink, 2013; Gabb, 2008).

Notwithstanding our sociological imperative, in the following chapters we have resisted the splintering of relationships into discrete objects of analysis and the definition of couples through their composition (e.g. same-sex/heterosexual, parents/childfree) or through prescriptive dimensions of dys/functionality that pathologise behaviour as under- or over-functioning. The deployment of such typologies, we maintain, serves to efface the multidimensionality of lived lives and the sets of contexts, predispositions and lifestyles that combine in myriad ways to form and reform these diverse relationships. They equally elide the ways couple relationships are underpinned by interwoven emotional, spatio-temporal and financial resources. We therefore situate our discussion in each of the chapters in the context of demographic information when this is relevant, but we do not describe participants in the *Enduring Love?* study through this. That is to say, we do not identify quotations through gender, sexual orientation, parental status and age unless this information is of particular pertinence to the point being raised. Parenthood is crucial in shaping couple experience, but it does not inexorably define the couple. The significance of gender slips in and out of focus. Heteronormative readings of the data should also be resisted as the queerest of couples may be the most traditional in form, and vice versa.

In Chapter 2, we examine how ideas of working at a relationship are now embedded within wider sets of social relationships and discourses in contemporary Britain. Our primary emphasis is on the relationship work that couples do, and the ways they understand what they do in the context of relationship work. The chapter moves, then, beyond analyses of the perceived drudgeries of domestic, emotional and reproductive labour and policy imperatives around 'successful' or 'better' relationships. By drawing together quantitative and qualitative data we identify the different forms of relationship practice ordinarily undertaken and which are all too often taken for granted or go unnoticed.

For many couples, the primary mode of relationship work which they recognise as important is communication. Whether relationships are open and disclosing or deploy strategies of not talking and silence, couples have often worked at establishing the most effective practices of communication for them. In Chapter 3, we focus on the meanings and impacts of what is said and unsaid including how the meanings and experience of love are operationalised and materialised. Communication is also often crucial in managing conflict and in our study, arguments were highlighted as one of the key things that couples disliked in their relationship. In this chapter, therefore, we explore how couples manage conflict. While arguments are often seen as destructive, in contrast, fond banter, laughter and humour are seen as positive dimensions in the couple's communication repertoire.

The focus in Chapter 4 is sex and intimacy. We interrogate how sex is experienced in couple relationships and the diverse range of intimate modes of expression. Overall, sex tends to be perceived as part of couple intimacy but not the intimate tie that connects the couple together. Our focus here, therefore, is not on sex acts per se, that is to say what couples 'do in bed' (or elsewhere); instead, we examine the meanings of sex and how sexual intimacy and physical affection, as relationship practices, are negotiated and experienced by partners. There is often notable divergence between partners in their sexual desire, and fluctuations in desire are typically adversely affected by age and parenthood, with gendered differences often framing the accounts presented. The 'success' and longevity of relationships in these circumstances seems to be couples' capacity to negotiate such circumstances. Practices are wide-ranging and designed around the particular needs of each couple and the individual partners within the couple, but a common thread that emerged in our findings is the positioning of such 'issues' as temporary phases that would not last forever. In so doing, couples are able to see beyond immediate constraints that get in the way of intimacy and intimate couple time.

In Chapter 5, we interrogate cultural ideas of coupledom, demonstrating how these fail to reflect lived experience and relationship diversity. We examine the nature and practices of 'triadic' relationships, reorienting how we perceive relationships and who affectively counts. In so doing, 'the sexual' is decentred as the primary determinant of the triad – a shift in emphasis that facilitates exploration of the rich fabric of couples' emotional and intimate networks which often include friends, pets, deities and, for some, other sexual partners. The chapter seeks, therefore, to demonstrate the complexity of couple relationships and to question notions of 'typical' experiences, the 'average' couple and 'the couple norm'. It contests the stratification of relationships into distinct relationship types and instead focuses on the ways in which different kinds of relationship practice cut across categorical differences such as generation, sexuality, parenting/partnering. Through an examination of the practices of 'couple displays', we conclude the chapter with an analysis of the boundaries and diversity of contemporary couple experience.

In the concluding chapter, we reassert the value of a practices approach to researching long-term couple relationships in twenty-first century Britain and highlight the complementary insights afforded by an examination of the spatio-temporal contexts in which relationship practices are situated. Through these contexts, we bring together our findings to focus on the mundane nature of relationship work undertaken by couples, the different meanings of loving and being loved in contemporary times and the importance of home for the ways in which couples are able to relate to each other. Through these foci, the chapter demonstrates how the *Enduring Love?* study extends and enhances understandings of the meanings and experiences of relationships and, at the same time, illustrates couples' resistance to, and strategies for, negotiating the powerful and pervasive cultural ideals of finding 'the one' and living 'happily ever after'.

Notes

1. Full details about the *Enduring Love?* study can be found in Appendix 1.
2. See Appendix 1 for detailed discussion of these methods.

References

Askham, J. (1984). *Identity and Stability in Marriage*. Cambridge: Cambridge University Press.

Back, L. (2007). *The Art of Listening*. Oxford and New York: Berg.

Barker, M., Gill, R., & Harvey, L. (2015). *Mediated Intimacy: Sex Advice in Media Culture*. London: Polity Press.

Bawin-Legros, B. (2004). Intimacy and the New Sentimental Order. *Current Sociology, 52*(2), 241–250.

BBC4 (Writer). (2012). *Love and Marriage: A 20th Century Romance* [Television series]. Retrieved 10 September 2014, from http://www.bbc.co.uk/programmes/b01msfkl

Beaumont, J. (2011). *Households and Families, Social Trends 41*. London: Office for National Statistics.

Beck, U., & Beck-Gernsheim, E. (1995). *The Normal Chaos of Love*. Cambridge: Polity Press.

Bell, C., & Newby, H. (1976). Husbands and Wives. In D. Leonard & S. Allen (Eds.), *Dependence and Exploitation in Work and Marriage*. London: Longman.

Berlant, L. (2012). *Desire/Love*. Brooklyn, NY: Punctum Books.

Blood, R. O., & Wolfe, D. M. (1960). *Husbands and Wives*. Glencoe, IL: Free Press.

Blyth, C. (2010). *The Art of Marriage*. London: John Murray.

Brownlie, J. (2014). *Ordinary Relationships: A Sociological Study of Emotions, Reflexivity and Culture*. Basingstoke: Palgrave Macmillan.

Budgeon, S. (2008). Couple Culture and the Production of Singleness. *Sexualities, 11*(3), 301–316.

Butler, M. H., Gardner, B. C., & Bird, M. H. (1998). Not Just a Time-Out: Change Dynamics of Prayer for Religious Couples in Conflict Situations. *Family Process, 37*(4), 451–478.

Chang, Y.-S., & Barrett, H. (2009). *Couple Relationships: A Review of the Nature and Effectiveness of Support Services*. London: Family and Parenting Institute.

Chapman, G. (2010). *The Five Love Languages: The Secret to Love That Lasts*. Chicago, IL: Northfield Publishing.

Clark, D. (Ed.). (1991). *Marriage, Domestic Life and Social Change*. London: Routledge.

Coleman, L., & Glenn, F. (2009). *When Couples Part*. London: OnePlusOne Publications.

Coleman, L., & Glenn, F. (2010). The Varied Impact of Couple Relationship Breakdown on Children: Implications for Policy and Practice. *Children and Society, 24*(3), 238–249.

CSJ. (2013). *Supporting Families, Strengthening Marriage: A Plan for a Meaningful Transferable Tax Allowance for Married Couples*. London: Centre for Social Justice.

CSJ. (2014a). *Family Breakdown*. Retrieved 31 August 2014, from http://www.centreforsocialjustice.org.uk/policy/pathways-to-poverty/family-breakdown

CSJ. (2014b). *Fully Committed? How a Government Could Reverse Family Breakdown*. London: Centre for Social Justice.

Daly, K. J. (2003). Family Theory versus the Theories Families Live by. *Journal of Marriage and Family, 65*(4), 771–784.

DfCSF. (2007). *Every Parent Matters*. London: HMSO.

DfCSF. (2010). *Support for All: Families and Relationships*. London: HMSO.

DfES. (2003). *Every Child Matters*. London: HMSO.

Duck, S. (2007). *Human Relationships*. London: Sage.

Duncan, S., & Phillips, M. (2008). New Families? Tradition and Change in Modern Relationships. In A. Park, J. Curtice, K. Thomson, M. Phillips, M. Johnson, & E. Clery (Eds.), *British Social Attitudes: The 24th Report*. London: Sage.

Duncombe, J., & Marsden, D. (1995). Can Men Love? 'Reading', 'Staging' and 'Resisting' the Romance. In L. Pearce & J. Stacey (Eds.), *Romance Revisited*. London: Lawrence & Wishart.

Edgell, S. (1980). *Middle Class Couples*. London: Allen and Unwin.

Eldén, S. (2011). The Threat or Promise of Popular Therapy? A Feminist Reading of Narratives of 'The Good Couple'. *NORA – Nordic Journal of Feminist Research, 19*(3), 144–162.

Ferri, E., & Smith, K. (2003). Family Life. In E. Ferri, J. Bynner, & M. Wadsworth (Eds.), *Changing Britain, Changing Lives: Three Generations at the Turn of the Century*. London: Institute of Education Press.

Figes, K. (2010). *Couples. The Truth*. London: Virago.

Fink, J. (2013). 'They Don't Really Care What Happens to Me': Divorce, Family Life and Children's Emotional Worlds in 1950s' British Cinema. In V. Cvetkovic & D. Olson (Eds.), *Portrayals of Children in Popular Culture: Fleeting Images* (pp. 153–169). New York: Lexington Books.

Fink, J., & Lomax, H. (2014). Challenging Images? Dominant, Residual and Emergent Meanings in on-Line Media Representations of Child Poverty. *Journal for the Study of British Cultures, 21*(1), 79–95.

Fitzpatrick, M. A. (1988). *Between Husbands and Wives: Communication in Marriage*. London: Sage.

Fraser, A. (2010). *Must You Go? My Life with Harold Pinter*. London: Weidenfeld and Nicolson.

Furedi, F. (2004). *Therapy Culture: Cultivating Vulnerability in an Uncertain Age*. London: Routledge.

Gabb, J. (2008). *Researching Intimacy in Families*. Basingstoke: Palgrave Macmillan.

Gabb, J. (2009). Researching Family Relationships: A Qualitative Mixed Methods Approach. *Methodological Innovations Online, 4*(2), 37–52.

Gabb, J. (2011). Family Lives and Relational Living: Taking Account of Otherness. *Sociological Research Online, 16*(4). Retrieved from http://www.socresonline.org.uk/16/14/10.html

Giddens, A. (1992). *The Transformation of Intimacy: Sexuality, Love and Eroticism in Modern Societies*. Cambridge: Polity Press.

Gottlieb, L. (2010). *Mr. Good Enough*. London: Collins.

Heaphy, B. (2009). Choice and Its Limits in Older Lesbian and Gay Narratives of Relational Life. *Journal of GLBT Family Studies, 5*(1/2), 119–138.

Heaphy, B., Smart, C., & Einarsdottir, A. (2013). *Same Sex Marriages: New Generations, New Relationships*. Basingstoke: Palgrave Macmillan.

Hird, M., & Abshoff, K. (2000). Women without Children: A Contradiction in Terms? *Journal of Comparative Family Studies, 31*(3), 347–361.

Hockey, J., Meah, A., & Robinson, V. (2010). *Mundane Heterosexualities: From Theory to Practices*. Basingstoke: Palgrave Macmillan.

Hodgkins, J. (2012). *Amateurs in Eden: The Story of a Bohemian Marriage*. London: Virago.

Hooff, J. v. (2013). *Modern Couples? Continuity and Change in Heterosexual Relationships*. London: Ashgate.

Illouz, E. (2012). *Why Love Hurts*. Cambridge: Polity Press.

Jackson, S. (1993). Even Sociologists Fall in Love: An Exploration in the Sociology of Emotions. *Sociology, 27*(2), 201–220.

Jackson, S., & Scott, S. (2004). Sexual Antinomies in Late Modernity. *Sexualities, 7*(2), 233–248.

Jackson, S., & Scott, S. (2007). Faking Like a Woman? Towards an Interpretive Theorization of Sexual Pleasure. *Body & Society, 13*(2), 95–116.

Jamieson, L. (1998). *Intimacy: Personal Relationships in Modern Societies*. Cambridge: Polity Press.

Jamieson, L. (1999). Intimacy Transformed? A Critical Look at the 'Pure' Relationship. *Sociology, 33*(3), 477–494.

Jamieson, L. (2005). Boundaries of Intimacy. In L. McKie & S. Cunningham-Burley (Eds.), *Families in Society. Boundaries and Relationships* (pp. 189–206). Bristol: The Policy Press.

Jamieson, L. (2011). Intimacy as a Concept: Explaining Social Change in the Context of Globalisation or Another Form of Ethnocentricism? *Sociological Research Online, 16*(4). Retrieved from http://www.socresonline.org.uk/16/14/15.html

Jamieson, L., Morgan, D., Crow, G., & Allan, G. (2006). Friends, Neighbours and Distant Partners: Extending or Decentring Family Relationships?

Sociological Research Online, 11(3). Retrieved from http://www.socresonline. org.uk/11/13/jamieson.html

Johnson, A. (1996). 'It's Good to Talk': The Focus Group and the Sociological Imagination. *Sociological Review, 44*, 517–538.

Koropeckyj-Cox, T., & Pendell, G. (2007). The Gender Gap in Attitudes about Childlessness in the United States. *Journal of Marriage and the Family, 69*(4), 899–915.

Kouneski, E. F., & Olson, D. H. (2004). A Practical Look at Intimacy. In D. Mashek & A. Aron (Eds.), *Handbook of Closeness and Intimacy* (pp. 117–133). Mahwah, NJ: Lawrence Erlbaum.

Langhamer, C. (2013). *The English in Love: The Intimate Story of an Emotional Revolution.* Oxford: Oxford University Press.

Lawrence, E., Rothman, A. D., Cobb, R. J., Rothman, M. T., & Bradbury, T. N. (2008). Marital Satisfaction across the Transition to Parenthood. *Journal of Family Psychology, 22*(1), 41–50.

Lewis, J. (2001). *The End of Marriage?* Cheltenham: Edward Elgar.

Lindqvist, B. (1996). It's All about Love: Conversations about Marriage and Career. In J. Frykman & O. Löfgren (Eds.), *Force of Habit: Exploring Everyday Culture* (pp. 47–58). Lund: Lund University Press.

Mansfield, P., & Collard, J. (1988). *The Beginning of the Rest of Your Life?* London: Macmillan.

Markham, H. J., & Halford, W. K. (2005). International Perspectives on Couple Relationship Education. *Family Process, 44*(2), 139–146.

Marsden, D. (1990). *The Social Construction of Coupledom.* ESRC (R000232737).

Mashek, D., & Aron, A. (Eds.). (2004). *Handbook of Closeness and Intimacy.* Mahwah, NJ: Lawrence Erlbaum Associates.

Mason, J. (2011). Facet Methodology: The Case for an Inventive Research Orientation. *Methodological Innovations Online, 6*(3), 75–92.

McCarthy, J. R., Gillies, V., & Holland, J. (2003). Multiple Perspectives on the 'Family' Lives of Young People: Methodological and Theoretical Issues in Case Study Research. *International Journal of Social Research Methodology, 6*(1), 1–23.

Montemurro, B. (2014). Getting Married, Breaking Up and Making Up for Lost Time: Relationship Transitions as Turning Points in Women's Sexuality. *Journal of Contemporary Ethnography, 43*(1), 64–93.

Morgan, D. H. J. (1996). *Family Connections: An Introduction to Family Studies.* Cambridge: Polity Press.

Morgan, D. H. J. (2011). *Rethinking Family Practices.* Basingstoke: Palgrave Macmillan.

NATSAL. (2013). *The Third National Survey of Sexual Attitudes and Lifestyles.* The Lancet. Retrieved from http://www.thelancet.com/themed/natsal.

Neustatter, A. (2012). *A Home for the Heart: 11 Ideas to Balance Your Life.* London: Gibson Square Books.

O'Hara, M. (2014). *Austerity Bites. A Journey to the Sharp End of Cuts in the UK.* Bristol: The Policy Press.

ONS. (2011). *Civil Partnerships in the UK, 2010, Statistical Bulletin.* Newport: ONS.

ONS. (2012). *Divorces in England and Wales – 2011. Statistical Bulletin.* Retrieved from http://www.ons.gov.uk/ons/dcp171778_291750.pdf

ONS. (2014). *9 Facts About Marriages.* Retrieved 8 September 2014, from http://www.ons.gov.uk/ons/rel/vsob1/marriages-in-england-and-wales–provisional-/2012/sty-marriage-facts.html

Peel, E., & Harding, R. (2008). Recognizing and Celebrating Same-Sex Relationships: Beyond the Normative Debate. *Sexualities, 11*(6), 659–666.

Phoenix, A., & Brannen, J. (2013). Researching Family Practices in Everyday Life: Methodological Reflections from Two Studies. *International Journal of Social Research Methodology, 17*(1), 11–26.

Pink, S. (2012). *Situating Everyday Life: Practices and Places.* London: Sage.

Plummer, K. (2003). *Intimate Citizenship: Private Decisions and Public Dialogues.* Seattle and London: University of Washington Press.

Ramazanoglu, C., & Holland, J. (2002). *Feminist Methodology: Challenges and Choices.* London: Sage.

Reibstein, J. (2006). *The Best Kept Secret.* London: Bloomsbury.

Relationships Alliance. (2013). The Relationships Alliance. *Priorities for Policy.* Retrieved 8 September 2014, from http://www.relate.org.uk/files/relate/publication-relationships-alliance-priorities-2013.pdf

Relationships Alliance. (2014). *The Relationships Manifesto: Strengthening Relationships.* Retrieved 29 October 2014, from http://www.relate.org.uk/files/relate/ramanifestoprint.pdf

Robinson, V. (2003). Problematic Proposals: Marriage and Cohabitation. *Feminism & Psychology, 13*(4), 437–441.

Roseneil, S. (2006). The Ambivalences of Angel's 'Arrangement': A Psychosocial Lens on the Contemporary Condition of Personal Life. *The Sociological Review, 54*(4), 847–869.

Roseneil, S., & Budgeon, S. (2004). Cultures of Intimacy and Care beyond 'the Family': Personal Life and Social Change in the Early 21st Century. *Current Sociology, 52*(2), 135–159.

Sherwood, C., Kneale, D., & Bloomfield, B. (2014). *The Way We Are Now: The UK's Relationships 2014*. London: Relate.

Shove, E., Pantzar, M., & Watson, M. (2012). *The Dynamics of Social Practice: Everyday Life and How It Changes*. London: Sage.

Silva, E. B., & Smart, C. (Eds.). (1999). *The New Family?* London: Sage.

Smart, C. (2007). *Personal Life*. Cambridge: Polity Press.

Smith, A. M. (2007). *Welfare Reform and Sexual Regulation*. Cambridge: Cambridge University Press.

Stacey, J. (2011). *Unhitched: Love, Marriage, and Family Values from West Hollywood to Western China*. New York: New York University Press.

Stewart, K. (2007). *Ordinary Affects*. Durham, NC: Duke University Press.

Walker, J., Barrett, H., Wilson, G., & Chang, Y.-S. (2010). *Understanding the Needs of Adults (Particularly Parents) Regarding Relationship Support. Research Brief DCSF-RBX-10-01*. London: DCFS.

Walkerdine, V. (1998). *Daddy's Girl: Young Girls and Popular Culture*. Cambridge, MA: Harvard University Press.

Waller, M. (2010). *The English Marriage: Tales of Love, Money and Adultery*. London: John Murray.

Wilkinson, E. (2013). Learning to Love Again: 'Brosken Families', Citizenship and the State Promotion of Coupledom. *Geoforum, 49,* 206–213.

Williams, F. (2004). *Rethinking Families. Moral Tales of Parenting and Step-Parenting*. London: Calouste Gulbenkian Foundation.

2

Relationship Work

The starting point for our analysis in this chapter is the provocation of Laura Kipnis (2004) that, because long-term couple relationships require such constant maintenance to succeed, they are ill-suited to contemporary lifestyles and ways of loving. Her argument is that monogamy is hard work; desire is 'organized contractually, with accounts kept and fidelity extracted like labor from employees'; and marriage is 'a domestic factory policed by means of rigid shop-floor discipline designed to keep the wives and husbands of the world choke-chained to the reproduction machinery' (Kipnis, 2004, p. 294). This process is so labour-intensive and statistically prone to failure that by definition, she argues, both marriage and couple-dom are not working. Kipnis' critique of marriage thus draws heavily on ideas of relationship work in ways that mirror our own analytical focus, albeit our respective interpretations of the experience and meanings of relationship work sit in contra-distinction. She does, however, accurately point to the emphasis in couple counselling and therapy on the need to work on the couple project for a relationship to 'succeed'. Indeed, as we highlighted in Chapter 1, the socio-cultural and political contexts in which couple relationships have become increasingly embedded in and imagined through have placed particular emphasis, in recent years, on

© The Author(s) 2018
J. Gabb, J. Fink, *Couple Relationships in the 21st Century*, Palgrave Macmillan Studies in Family and Intimate Life, DOI 10.1007/978-3-319-59698-3_2

the importance of working at relationships, relationships that work and supporting couples to make their relationships work better.

Like Kipnis (1998), our analysis takes a long view, drawing on nineteenth-century theories of labour and capital, twentieth-century feminist critiques of domestic labour, emotion work and reproductive labour as well as more recent therapeutic arguments that good marriages take work. The focus is on the everyday practices that couples do to sustain their relationships and the material conditions that shape their personal lives. Our conceptualisation of relationship work thus inculcates ideas of work and capital while keeping a keen eye on the intensity of emotions. We situate the term in the context of writing on emotion work and the economies of gratitude (for an overview see Gabb, 2008, pp. 90–93). Here, studies of the economy of intimacy (Zelizer, 2005), the gendering of emotion work (Duncombe & Marsden, 1993; Hochschild, 1979, 1989) and the affective economy of gratitude (Hochschild, 2003) explore the intersections of public–private worlds. For Arlie Hochschild (1989), women's 'gift' of emotion work entrenches the distinctive roles of women and men and is crucial to maintaining the economy of families:

An economy of gratitude is a vital, nearly sacred, nearly bottom-most, largely implicit layer of an intimate bond. It is the summary of all *felt gifts*. (Hochschild, 2003, p. 105)

Personal and symbolic meanings afforded to gift exchanges serve to sustain them and render them meaningful within their broader social contexts. For example, a woman may feel grateful for the gift of additional childcare contributions 'given' by her husband, but if roles were reversed, such activities would not constitute a gift as they constitute part of women's traditional role in the family. Analysing couple relationships through the lens of emotion work thus serves to facilitate insight into the social meanings and values attached to gendered intimate exchanges. Similarly, although our analysis is largely focused on the ways in which relationship work undertaken by couples ordinarily features in the home, we are also able to trace how it extends beyond the boundaries of the household and personal life. For example, as Emma illustrates, with the shift from a male breadwinner/female housewife model of couple relationships, establishing a successful career for either partner or keeping the work–family life scales balanced has to be a joint endeavour. Here, the gift of support and kindness is seen as central.

Emma: I was applying for job after job, but he helped me through that in every way that he possibly could have done […] On the day of the interview as well […] he went to the organic food shop and bought me some really nice porridge to make me breakfast in the morning […] He just did everything that he could have possibly done to make the day not stressful for me, and sort of walked me to the bus stop in the rain, and things like that.

Although gender roles and inequalities do often remain embedded and intransigent in couple relationships, in the *Enduring Love?* study women and men, heterosexual and LGBQ not only appeared to accept that relationships take work but also appreciated, cherished and, at times, even relished the mundane emotional and practical labour required to sustain their relationships. Relationship work was not perceived negatively as onerous work but as part and parcel of being in a relationship. Working together through tough times was seen as an investment that could strengthen the relationship.

Thomas: The tough times that you get in marriages can, I think if you handle them right, can … can strengthen your marriage. So like death of … death of family member or parents which we both experienced […] death of children which, we had a miscarriage […] those types of things can cause great stresses on marriage and sometimes you hear that they are, they were the root of what caused the marriage to fall down. So you, I think you have to work hard at it.

As we noted in Chapter 1, research has shown that couple relationships come under immense pressure in times of transition and stress, and that these factors can contribute to relationship breakdown (ONS, 2012; Walker et al., 2010). Our findings suggest that stressors are commonplace and that there may be, in counter fact, a significant *positive* correlation between stressful events experienced and relationship satisfaction (Gabb, Klett-Davies, Fink, & Thomae, 2013). Our analysis thus provides new insight on the prevalence and impact of stressful experiences in couple relationships. Such experiences remind us that emotional 'ups and downs' and changes in life circumstances are part of all couple relationships, to different degrees and at different points in time.

Miscarriage, for example, was a recurrent and particularly poignant example that was mentioned by a number of the couples in our study. The emotion work needed to mutually support each other through this time, and thereafter, was identified as a bittersweet element of the couple relationship.

Debs: When we lost the baby, we decided that we wanted to do some kind of symbolic, you know, ceremony, a kind of grieving ceremony. And we invited just a few very closest family and friends and we'd already decided to plant a tree which is flourishing […] I think most of the ideas came from him. I mean we did ask the people to suggest things and I think several of them said poems, said, you know, poems and things. But the actual acts, the kind of symbolic acts, I think that was nearly all [partner …] and I just feel … [emotional and a little choked with tears)] I feel so blessed I suppose to use a religious word […] But it feels like such a gift from [partner] when he can do that. Particularly because I don't expect him to do that [… it was] just a real gift from him to me that [emotional and tearful] was really meaningful, yeah. And that was so unexpected, even though once he'd done it for the baby we lost, I was … I kind of, we'd already had a conversation where I'd gone, 'You're really good at this' and he'd gone, 'Yes I am aren't I, it's really surprising' but you know … but we're still both surprised […] we did a little mini … the date that the first baby was due, we deliberately went on holiday to be away over that period […] I think we just lit a few candles and there was some rosemary growing on the [holiday cottage], so we, you know, rosemary for remembrance [emotional and tearful] and that kind of thing … so yes, that kind of, yeah marking the transitions.

The pain in Debs' account remains visceral and raw. The couple now have two children but the feelings experienced during the time of the miscarriage are still etched on both her and her partner. Working through this time, acknowledging their individual and shared feelings and marking the anniversary of their loss have, however, enabled their partnership to feel stronger. It also facilitated Debs' partner to realise relationship skills and a dimension of himself that were hitherto unexplored. The rituals that surrounded the miscarriage have thus had a lasting affirming impact on their long-term relationship, and their shared comfort in the commemoration event has now been translated into celebrations of the birth dates of the children and other significant relationship markers.

Gifts and thoughtful gestures

For Debs and her partner, working together to find a way through their grief included emotion work that was perceived and experienced as a 'gift'. Similar acts of kindness, generosity of thought and compassion were identified in answers in our online survey in response to the open free-text question 'What does your partner do that makes you feel appreciated?'[1] For example, surprise gifts, thoughtful gestures and the stand-alone gesture of a cup of tea and/or breakfast in bed were highly valued. Indeed, when combined, these comprised the most popular response and, as such, they are grouped together here, in this chapter, to explore some of the relationship work being ordinarily undertaken by couples. Across this diverse array of everyday practices, the quality or value of a gesture was seldom dependent on money; it was, instead, the intimate *couple knowledge* which these manifested that really counted. From scraping the ice off a car to taking the dog out for a walk in the wind and rain, it was a partner undertaking mundane routine tasks that was identified as kind and considerate:

> Takes out the bins and always clearing up after dinner
> Gives me time to relax when I get home from work

To reiterate, responses such as these were to *free-text* questions. That is to say, from all the available thoughts, gestures and practices that could have been identified, it was mundanities which appeared to be most highly prized. Domestic roles and responsibilities thus rested alongside a sense of commitment and togetherness. Sometimes providing much-needed care and support, at other times gestures were simply unexpected acts of kindness which made the partner feel loved and cared for. When tangible objects such as gifts, cards and flowers were specifically mentioned, it was typically the thoughtfulness behind the gesture that was most appreciated:

> Every year he brings me an orange rose from a garden that he maintains

Romance was thus present in the giving and receiving of gifts, but commercialised formulations of the romantic gesture were seldom mentioned. Indeed, it was the commemoration of time spent together and the marking of the relationship *over time* that was typically most cherished, as the annual gift of the single orange rose illustrates. Other descriptions also applauded the spontaneity of thoughtful acts and practices:

> Surprising me with such things as a nice bath, cuppa, favourite TV show or film at just the right time

A cup of tea (and, to a lesser extent, a mug of coffee and/or breakfast in bed), while being a thoughtful gesture among many others, featured so prominently as an answer in the survey that it was identified as a sub-theme and assigned an individual code. Many responses in this vein were almost apologetic in their phrasing, while others clearly identified this small act of generosity as the way their partner expressed their love and appreciation, ideas that we explore more fully in Chapter 3. The proverbial 'cuppa' is iconic in British culture. Its value, therefore, draws on both its cultural status and personal meaning. For mothers who responded to the survey, the pleasures of being brought a cup of tea in bed were often closely associated with time out, away from the demands of childcare and signified their partner's appreciation of both them and their maternal role. As such this *silent* gesture *spoke* volumes (Gabb, 2013).

> A cup of tea in bed every now and again makes you feel so appreciated
> Takes kids out without me, brings me cup of tea in bed in mornings

The symbolic value of this gesture within the parental economy might therefore account for why childless men seldom mentioned this item, findings which reaffirm the importance of parenthood (Coleman, 2011) and gender (Langford, 1999) in shaping couple relationship experience. There is thus an acknowledgement and valuing of the everyday mundanities that go into relationship work and that are required for a relationship to sustain over time. Such endeavours were appreciated as relationship 'gifts': *acts of reciprocity* that bound the couple together through give and take.

Household chores and childcare

Couple relationships endure for many diverse reasons, including the strength of a connection, the intimacy of the partnership bond, an intensity of feelings or a sense of 'deep knowing' (Jamieson, 1998). These emotional dimensions featured in many of the survey responses thus far identified as gestures which one partner does to make the other feel appreciated. There is another category of answers which stands apart from these and which is perhaps far more mundane. Sharing household chores and childcare was identified as crucial in sustaining a family, a household and thus the couple relationship.

> He vacuum cleans the house, he knows I hate it. Helps around the house and with the kids
> We have a new baby. He will take him in the morning to let me sleep

Similar responses featured in answers to the other two open questions, 'What do you like best about your relationship?' and 'What do you like least about your relationship?'[2] Feminist research has demonstrated the need to recognise the distinctiveness of household labour and the roles and responsibilities associated with childcare (Klett-Davies & Skaliotis, 2009). Responses in this vein were, however, so often interwoven that this distinction became untenable (Oakley, 2005). Mothers were unsurprisingly far more inclined to rate the sharing of household chores and childcare as a priority. However, as we indicated in Chapter 1, these responses should be seen in the context of existing research on the gendering of assessments around household labour (Doucet, 1995) which has shown that women are likely to notice and disproportionately appreciate small amounts of household chores and childcare (Coltrane, 1996; Hochschild, 1989). As such, we might infer that these responses say as much about gender norms as they do about domesticity and couple relationship practices. Indeed, the sort of labour identified by survey respondents was often deeply gendered, particularly around what was expected and appreciated. While both women and men did appear to genuinely recognise the underpinning value of the everyday mundanities that go into relationship work, fathers tended to articulate feeling appreciated through gratitude for the emotional and practical support which *they personally received*, more than that provided to support the family and household more generally.

> She looks after me … washing up, cooking, etc.

This personal support which fathers receive may enable them to function more effectively both inside and outside the home. This finding has the flavour of a study that was written 30 years ago (Finch, 1983), which asserts that when a woman marries she takes more on than a husband; her life becomes structured by his occupation and more likely than not she will be drawn into it to some degree. Thus, if she is also employed, a woman will do not two but three jobs: hers, theirs (managing household and childcare responsibilities) and some of his as well. That is to say, she facilitates his labour power through the emotional work of moral support (Hochschild, 1989). Qualitative data from our study presents perhaps a more complicated picture of how the domestic division of labour operates as relationship work. Interestingly, in many ways, it represented an economy of exchange which brought with it mutual personal rewards and also realigned gendered understandings of fairness and equality.

Zak: Shopping was like, became evidence of my usefulness to the relationship. Because we'd go shopping, [my partner] would do the wandering and pick everything out and I'd go with her and we'd talk and banter as we do, but when we come to bringing everything home, I would load up with virtually everything and carry it all myself. That's … that would be the self-worth. I'm strong, strong, I'm useful, I'm carrying everything so you don't have to.

As this interview extract indicates, the weekly shopping trip, with its accompanying talk and banter, offers Zak and his partner an opportunity to connect emotionally with each other. For both these young people with busy full-time careers, this opportunity is most welcome. The activity also serves a secondary and individually important function in that it provides Zak with 'evidence' that he is needed; his physical strength and his capacity to make the drudgery of shopping a more pleasurable experience for both of them is thus self-fulfilling. Note the subtle shift of personal pronouns in the extract, which start with '*we*'d go shopping'; '*we*'d talk and banter'; '*we* come to bringing everything home' and then switch to '*I* would load up'; '*I'm* strong'; '*I'm* useful'; '*I'm* carrying everything'. By identifying shopping as relationship work rather than domestic labour, it is therefore possible to tease out how Zak uses shopping to maintain his masculine identity and thus materially and symbolically occupy a useful role in the relationship. In this way the meanings of the gendered nature of Zak's relationship work can be seen as serving to bolster his seemingly fragile sense of self through the enactment of his masculine role, while also facilitating the sharing of, and enjoyment in, performing necessary routine domestic activities.

For other men in the study, however, relationship work offered them an opportunity to manage their gender identities in ways which resisted dominant norms of masculinity. Duncan suggested that with age and maturity he had come to a greater understanding of himself and at the same time an appreciation of the work undertaken by his partner that allowed him to be himself.

Duncan: Well, I think because we're both second time around, we are very aware of the pitfalls, and things that didn't work in the past etc., I've learnt a lot since my first marriage … I think the biggest thing for me is that my partner lets me be me; I've never had that before. I've always felt that I've not been forced,

> but been required to be something that didn't sit well with
> me. So I think I am very happy with the way things are
> because of that, you know, little allowance that I get just to be
> me … I say little allowance, but it's a big thing, and I think,
> as I say, I've never had it before, and it's just brilliant.

Jamieson (1998) suggests that couples' intimate knowing and understanding of each other are not just cognitive but also emotional and sympathetic, in that a deep insight into an inner self is also demanded. For
Duncan, this work of deep knowing by his partner is not dependent on
the time that the couple have been together; theirs is not a *long* relationship. Rather, it builds on what they have learnt over time as individuals
and through their previous relationships. In participants' responses across
the qualitative and quantitative datasets, the meanings and experience
of being in a 'second' or 'third' long-term relationship appeared to be
often significant. For example, when responding to what makes them
feel appreciated, parents appeared to value a partner's childcare role more
highly if the partner was not the birth parent of the child/ren, or, in
the very least, they framed their appreciation through this differentiating characteristic: 'Looks after *my* son' (our emphasis). Being a 'second
time rounder' can therefore make the couple relationship *qualitatively*
different. Partners bring to the new relationship memories, experience,
legacies and emotional bruises of past lives and loves and these imprints
can incline greater degrees of couple reflexivity and/or a desire to do it
differently – or 'better' – next time around.

Cooking

As with childcare, cooking was embedded within survey responses around
household labour but we disaggregated activities around food and meal-
times both because of its frequency and to facilitate closer analysis of this
form of relationship work.

> She takes the time to prepare incredible meals that are also healthy
> He cooks my dinner for me so that I don't have to when I get home from
> work

Cooking was highly valued by women and men equally. Cooking dinner for a partner can be seen as literally and metaphorically *feeding the relationship*. Descriptions of these culinary activities suggested a real sense of appreciation for the time and energy devoted to domestic labour. Qualitative data again provide another layer of understanding and complexity which unsettles simple gendered readings. In these data the meanings of activities can be understood through a participant's 'relational biography' (Heaphy et al., 2013) and sense of self and identity (Szabo, 2014). For example, in one instance, shopping for groceries and cooking served as the scaffold for emerging sets of feelings that were expanding to include a third partner within the couple's open relationship. Culinary activities thus provided insight into how the triadic dynamic is being negotiated and experienced in different relational configurations. Here, the binary logic of 'the sexes' is broken down and a more nuanced appreciation of power and domesticity comes to the fore. This queering of housework and the emotional labour undertaken therein requires us to think beyond gender norms (Goldberg, 2013). We examine the meanings and experience of relationships which challenge the dyadic boundaries of coupledom in Chapter 5, but here, drawing on diary data from one of the men, we focus on the ways relationship work completed around food serves to nurture the emerging relationship dynamic and undo gender roles.

Andreas' diary recounts a seamless blend of sex, shopping trips and cooking, all of which appeared to be equally enjoyed. What these different activities facilitate is time alone, time together and time together apart by the individuals, the couple and the three men.

Andreas: After some very intense sex ... [lover] and [partner] went grocery shopping, and I stayed at home and listened to a song I found very fitting for my feelings

Within the spatial confines of their one bedroom flat and the emotional parameters of the relationship, Andreas is navigating a path that enables the relationship dynamic to grow while simultaneously protecting himself from the feelings that perhaps inevitably accompany such a shift in boundaries. The three-way sex is mutually enjoyed but so too is the subsequent time out, away from the immediate pressures of trying to work at the new relationship. This time affords him an emotional pause, where he can process his feelings; it also gives the other two men space to be alone together. The meal produced, with the food newly purchased, provides an occasion to bring the three of them together.

Andreas: After dinner we cuddled up on the couch and watched some funny videos on YouTube, finally watching an episode of Dr Who. We ate apple pie with custard, ([lover] likes his pie and his custard hot, [partner] likes his pie hot and his custard cold, and I like my pie and custard cold), and talked about this and that. I can't remember the contents of our conversation, but I enjoyed myself and I laughed a lot. Dr Who is simply weird.

What is described here, then, is a scene of domestic harmony as the men enjoy time together, building collective memories (through their TV viewing) and sharing a meal which is tailor-made to their own requirements. The attention to detail that Andreas affords to this moment, his individual care of each one's needs, demonstrates how seemingly mundane relationship work can materialise deeply meaningful 'affective practice' (Wetherell, 2012). But within this extract, and his data more generally, a sense of anxiety and uncertainty remains as the new relationship dynamic is established, making it work for all parties and safe for him. The attentive relationship work that is being undertaken in this culinary tailoring of apple pie and custard is thus deeply telling; it demonstrates Andreas' commitment to the relationship project but also the work that it is taking to meet everyone's different needs.

The meanings or even recognition of relationship work and its affective exchange value may not be immediately evident to either the outside world or even to those involved. Yet, once identified, the value of such practices becomes twofold, as *what they do* and *what they mean* combine. Such understandings were often facilitated through participation in the *Enduring Love?* study, affording personal insight and constituting a positive intervention in the couple relationship. For Sam and her partner, for example, the participatory methods of emotion maps and diaries provided them with a vehicle to think through various troubling dimensions

Figure 2.1 Toast and marmite

of their relationship, and also to acknowledge and celebrate the areas where things were working well. Here, in Sam's diary, the relationship work that she describes around food practices is beautifully illustrated – figuratively and analytically. Her completion of these data as such comprises another material form of the time and energies that she is investing in the couple relationship and their future together (Figure 2.1).

Sam: I got up and went to the shop for the newspaper ... I leave [partner] reading her book in bed. I come back and make [partner's] tea, my coffee and marmite on toast. I have a strange habit of always giving the best or most perfect toast to [partner] – I always take the worst of whatever it is for myself.

[Partner] must always have the best as she deserves it. If one bit of toast is a bit burnt or inferior to the other one in some way then that must be mine.

For Sam, making her partner breakfast in bed is a thoughtful gesture that communicates emotional volumes. The generosity of this act and her investment in this exchange are equally important. As with Andreas, Sam's attentiveness demonstrates both her desire to put her partner first, above herself, and her commitment to making the relationship work. In this relationship, where economic resources are scarce and, as we discuss later in the chapter, where internal and external factors combine to put pressure on the relationship, such gift exchanges are invaluable. The personal time that Sam devotes to this gesture is crucial, so too the couple time which this facilitates.

Couple time

As Sam illustrates, it is often time which defines relationship work and which characterises couples' investment in knowing and understanding each other. In Moira's account, for example, there is a particular emphasis on the early years of the couple relationship, perhaps because it was during this period that tensions existed between competing demands to build emotional connections with each other, establish their sense of self and identity and develop their respective professional careers.

Moira: We don't have to work too hard at it now, because we've been married over 30 years. We knew each other a couple of years before we got married, two, three years, and we met at university in our final year, so we've kind of grown up together really. And I would say in the first five, ten years we probably were working pretty hard at being together and being ourselves and, you know, launching our careers and living and you know, everything, so I think now it's a very nice position to be in when you think actually … we might have the occasional bicker but that's all it is.

Like Duncan (quoted earlier), Moira's experiences point to the satisfaction of deep knowing for her relationship and all that entails with regard to the cognitive, emotional and sympathetic relationship work that has been undertaken over many years. A related dimension of this dynamic of time and work is illustrated by Debs, who explains how the extent of relationship work that she and her partner have put in over many years together, has made their relationship now 'rich' enough to manage difficult periods.

Debs: The other thing that I think makes our relationship work, which we also have a metaphor for … is that it's like a bank account and that we go through periods when we're having a hard time … usually because of kind of external stuff, rather than fundamental problems in the relationship, we're just not getting enough sleep or you know one of the kids is being really horrible […] But, because our relationship feels so strong and has been going on for so long and we've been making deposits in it for so long, that's okay and we can kind of keep going, even with … not just not making deposits, but withdrawing … you know, it feels like we're withdrawing from the relationship, but it's alright because it doesn't run out of money.

In this context, therefore, relationship work can be clearly identified and understood through a related financial idea – 'saving for a rainy day'. As Debs says, their investment in the relationship, over time, serves to provide a buffer against unexpected events and challenges. Deposits in the relationship bank may be small, but, to exploit her financial metaphor further, their emotional compound interest is substantial.

Another important investment that was identified by this couple, and most, if not all others, was the *need* for time out from parenting. The everydayness of parenthood was occasionally held at bay through memories of earlier childfree lives and future times on the horizon, once children had grown up and left home. At other points, however, parenthood appeared to be simply overwhelming, as couples struggled to meet the pressing family demands of the here and now. Finding time away from parenthood was thus often hard work in itself, requiring them to wriggle through the cracks of over-filled schedules to *make time* for the couple. In talking about days off and nights in, the trope of 'date nights' was often mentioned, mirroring its emphasis in popular culture wherein spending quality time together is seen as an important relationship maintenance strategy that enables couples to stay connected. For some couples, like Jennie and Noel, such time provides a focus for their relationship work, a moment where small thoughtful gestures can be given and received, with pleasure and appreciation. As Jennie says in the couple interview:

> You cook on date night. You sometimes surprise me with a bottle of Coke or a bar of chocolate.

Date nights thus provided couples with an occasion for intimate 'quality time' together. For some couples this was quite ordinary and unstructured; for other couples it was strictly rule bound, to separate it from daily routines and make such time feel special and especially meaningful.

Genevieve: Date night – For a couple of months now [partner] + I have been trying to do 'date night' once a week. This is where we assign a night, often Thursday, + from around 8/9 have distraction-free time (no mobiles/laptops etc.), we watch a DVD or something on the TV (something relaxing + enjoyable), sometimes have a bath, and then go to bed in a relaxed mood with the hope that it leads to more … (not always but often does). This has really helped us as a couple – to make sure we have that quality relaxed time together each week + to keep the flame alive, so to speak!

Here, the crafting of date night is both negotiated and agreed on by the couple but it also draws on cultural repertoires of how to *do* quality couple time. For example, Genevieve intimates that date nights may be instrumentally used to rekindle sexual desire, something we discuss in Chapter 5. This couple is childfree; it is their otherwise busy lives and the lack of spontaneity therein which is being addressed through their proactive relationship work and decision to make time for their couple relationship. For parenting couples, the need or desire to establish couple time is often even greater, while the enormity and challenges of this feat can feel exponential. Young children are continually demanding. The bedtimes of teenage children make evening time alone seldom available. Adolescent awareness of sex means that parents' intimate life is no longer private because the symbolic meanings of closed bedroom doors are rendered meaningful (Gabb, 2008). For Christy and Thomas, for example, date nights have become infeasible now their children are older and so they instead take advantage of opportunities to spend moments together in the daytime, to simply catch up with each other.

Christy: Now the kids aren't in bed till half past nine, so that [a date night] doesn't quite work because then it's midnight by the time you get to bed, it's [laughter)] ... and you're knackered. So actually we're, yeah we're finding that if we have the same day off together, we'll go and do a day thing together [...]

Thomas: Yeah, even if you just grab a coffee or lunch together, it's just those small bits of time which just, you know.

Understandings of relationship work that were presented to us over and over again connect, then, to Carol Smart's argument about affirmations of love and commitment and the ways in which these are embedded in ordinary, everyday activities. Couple time invested and the relationship work completed 'may not appear "special" to the outside observer but are integral to the lives of the couple' (Smart, 2007, p. 68). This form of relationship work established the tenor through which couples came to live their lives together and through which they explained how their relationships have endured. In most cases, these lives and times were experienced in, and integral to, the crafting of home.

Home comforts

Relationship work was at times perceived as difficult by couples in our study, being curtailed and contained by circumstances that sometimes appeared to conspire against the couple. On other occasions, however, the investment of time was less arduous and the easiness of the moment made light work of the efforts required. Here, during evenings spent curled up on the sofa watching TV or listening to music, couple time served to instil a sense of being *at home*, comfortable in and comforted by the presence of a partner. In these instances, being together sometimes involved 'being silly' – a descriptor typically used with great fondness, involving occasions that were deeply treasured for their spontaneity and sense of fun. For Gareth and his partner, for example, it was the escalation of an ordinary day into an 'impromptu party' that made the time so special.

Gareth: In the afternoon we watched the end of *The West Wing* ... We basically drank quite heavily for the rest of the day! It's not that often that we have weekends off together at home especially when [partner] doesn't really have any work that needs doing urgently so it was really nice and relaxing. We started watching *Tinker Tailor Soldier Spy* in the evening, but were a bit too drunk to follow it, instead we ended up putting a load of music on and had a little impromptu party instead. Was a really fun day.

For couples who are time impoverished and resource poor, the pleasures of such a 'fun day' are all the sweeter. Many couples described occasions where they enjoyed watching TV and listening to music. The prevalence of dancing was, however, perhaps one of the most unexpected couple practices that we encountered. Its frequency demonstrated how this activity comprised a crucial part of the relationship work that some couples routinely do. For couples like Glen and his partner, where space, time and economic resources were scarce, it was arguably even more cherished because it enabled all the family to enjoy a good time together.

Glen: We were all cuddling each other and dancing and it was, like, really funny.

Dancing was used by couples in a variety of ways. It provided an opportunity for fun and frivolity, a moment of sensual intimacy or a space in which to hold at bay 'the blues'. The positive impact of dancing and movement in therapeutic contexts for those with mental health illnesses, such as depression, has been evidenced (Ernst, Rand, & Stevinson, 1998). Our research presents similar findings in the domestic context. In couples where mental health issues featured in shaping the relationship dynamic, the activity of dancing appeared to play an important role in their lives. Sam, for example, has a severe anxiety disorder; the couple live on benefits and provide care for an elderly relative. Their lives are not, therefore, always easy. Sam also identifies as transgender and had transitioned several years previously. Although the couple are very close and see each other as 'soul mates', this remains a source of unease for her partner. Dancing and 'being daft' provide this couple with a means to step out of their proverbial carpet slippers and resist the sedentary image that can sometimes contain long-term couples, especially those in later life. It also provides a way to celebrate both youthful histories (together and apart) and the continued pleasure they share in each other's company, and it builds some moments of light-heartedness into their lives in what are often otherwise testing circumstances (Figure 2.2).

Sam: We drink wine and watch [TV] … By the time that the [music] documentary finishes at 9.55, we are quite tipsy! WE LOVE [BAND]! WE HAVE ALL THEIR ALBUMS. DANCING MAKES US HAPPY … I put on the MiFi and we both dance to our favourite music … we went to bed very late! It was fun. I always have fun with [partner].

For this couple, dancing thus performs a vital relationship practice that serves to consolidate and strengthen their partnership. Music serves to *anchor* their relationship, as they sing along and dance to 'their tunes'. Their pleasure in this musical interlude is not restricted to the here and now but is part of the long-term couple narrative.

Activities such as listening to music or watching TV that are represented as 'down time' or even 'wasted time' in the social imaginary were often identified in the *Enduring Love?* study as deeply rewarding in sustaining a couple relationship through tough times and over the course of time more generally. Watching the same TV programmes was

Figure 2.2 Sam's emotion map

experienced by many couples as an important part of everyday couple life, with the routines and rhythms of such relationship practices being situated biographically, temporally and spatially.

Monica: When I was pregnant we got into *The Wire* and we watched endless, endless episodes … And it was a really intimate thing to do – to just sit there and be on the sofa together and watching a TV show.

In a letter to *The Guardian* on 7 November 2013, the Relationships Alliance (2013) pointed to the lack of available time for couples which could be devoted to their relationship. It highlighted that couples only spend about 150 minutes together per day, 50 minutes of which is spent watching TV. At the same time, Ofcom research (August 2013) points to a rise in multi-platform viewing and a return to family TV viewing, facilitated by large living room TV sets. The enjoyment *and rewards* of watching TV and DVD box sets are layered in meaning and were often perceived as a positive relationship practice by couples in our study. Such activities served to bring the couple together physically, sharing a space, often seated in close proximity or cuddled up together on the sofa, and provide another 'biographical anchor' (Heaphy et al., 2013) which enhanced their sense of togetherness.

For other couples, computer games performed a similarly cohesive function, providing time that was highly valued and deeply cherished because it offered an opportunity to escape humdrum work and domestic lives.

Jessica: After work today we decided to sit down and play a game that we'd enjoyed playing a long time ago, *The Legend of Zelda: Majora's Mask*. It's a fan-favourite game and we've both been looking forward to playing it like some people watch old films together. We ended up spending a whole evening on the sofa enjoying ourselves. It was a nice way to end a week of spending more time with each other.

Yet sharing multimedia activities was not always inextricably linked to couple time and intimacy. For some couples, it was the proximity of partners which counted rather than the sharing of an activity. Zak, for example, singled out being *together apart* as one aspect of his relationship that he particularly enjoyed.

Zak: I'm working my way through a video game with a story I enjoy. This means me + [partner] can engage in one of my preferred 'relationshippy' things, sitting in the same room, me playing, her watching a series on DVD. I don't mind this separation, although I draw the line at doing it in separate rooms.

Across the instances cited, therefore, what is crucial, we suggest, is the practice of shared time together and/or the sharing of time and space together apart. For others, however, ideas and everyday practices of being together apart were stretched to their limits. Here, TV preferences served to separate the couple. Time together was something to be avoided, or when encountered, an occasion fraught with tension and anxiety. Rosemary, for example, does a dance of a symbolic order with her husband, involving a highly choreographed orchestration as they move between rooms in order to spend as little time as possible together.

Rosemary: After lunch [partner] stayed in the front room whilst I stayed in the back sitting room doing my diary. I took over his seat in the front room as he's NOT very keen on what I watch on TV. We then swopped over rooms so [partner] could watch his TV show.

For this older couple, the 'dance' they do is an embodied arrangement which facilitates a shared, albeit unspoken solution to manage their daily lives, together apart. These deliberate manoeuvres enabled each party to enjoy individual pleasures and thus work to sustain their couple relationship.

For most couples, however, time apart and time alone were equally highly prized and actively sought out. The desire for 'me time' was not indicative of relationship dissatisfaction but was instead a crucial and positive dimension of the relationship work undertaken. In Chapter 5 we discuss in more detail responses to the survey question 'Who is the most important person in your life?' This question was included to interrogate the prevalence of individualisation as a defining characteristic of contemporary lives (Beck, 2000; Giddens, 1991). Suffice to say here that most people selected partner or child; but a notable proportion did select self, ranging from 5 to 17 per cent depending on residency and relationship status (Gabb et al., 2013). The participants who made this latter selection could easily be taken as the epitome of individualisation; indeed, the significance of independent living arrangements and differences between parental/childfree responses might predispose this inference. Their justification of their answers provides contra-evidence however, often situating the self *in relation* to others. The response was justified in terms of constancy, that is to say, in opposition to temporary and/or serial couple relationships. Looking after and valuing 'number one' was not characterised as selfishness, but was described as a means to provide the foundation for any relationships that might emerge. To look after a relationship and meet the needs and expectations of someone else requires a sense of personal robustness and security.

> Because if I can't look after myself, I can't look after anyone else
> My partner has greater needs than I do and our relationship feels more focused on meeting those, so I feel I need to look after myself so I am able to be there for her

In the study's qualitative data, responses in this vein similarly emphasised the benefits for the couple in nourishing the self. 'Me-time' included hobbies and individual friendships or simply taking 'time out' of the relationship to retain a personal and separate sense of one's own identity.

Kaylee: Being alone is something I love. I find a lot of peace when I am in silence. I find I am able to rest and to be with my 'self'. I am able to think. As much as I am active and like to explore the outside, I also like to be still. It is something I need and I always try to make sure I get some of it during the week.

The *indulgence* of 'me time' was often jealously protected and actively instigated by couples – whether, as discussed earlier, this took the form of 15 minutes out enjoying a cup of tea in bed, away from the children, or longer periods of time alone to think and reflect. Whatever its nature or purpose, such time was always deeply valued and identified as a crucial relationship practice that served to maintain the equilibrium of the couple dynamic.

In this chapter, we have sought to explore how couples work together, together apart and separately to sustain their relationships. Through this, we have unpicked the meanings and practices of the diverse range of relationship work which couples undertake, with an emphasis on deep knowing, investment, time time:and relationship work and commitment. Our findings, we suggest, blur the clear-cut distinctions ordinarily advanced through gender differences in, or gendered attitudes towards, the ways in which relationships are sustained. Participants in the *Enduring Love?* study, both women and men, valued and respected the different emotional, physical and practical dimensions of their *mutual relationship work* and the contribution that this made to the partnership dynamic and personal well-being. Throughout this analysis, the significance of time – both its quotidian demands and its cumulative effect, over decades – cannot be overstated, as illustrated so imaginatively by Debs' metaphor of the bank account. Nevertheless, as we have emphasised throughout, unlike domestic, emotional and reproductive labour, relationship work in and of itself need not be demanding or hard work. It is typically understood by couples as small gestures that embody thoughtfulness, kindness and care and, as such, is enjoyed and treasured in this momentary mundane form.

Notes

1. See Appendix 2, Table A2.1: 'What does your partner do for you that makes you feel appreciated?' For full details on the open free-text questions and how we analysed the data these generated, see Appendix 1.
2. See Appendix 2, Table A2.2: 'What do you like best about your relationship?' and Table A2.3: 'What do you like least about your relationship?' for a full breakdown of responses to these questions.

References

Beck, U. (2000). Living Your Own Life in a Runaway World: Individualization, Globalization and Politics. In W. Hutton & A. Giddens (Eds.), *On the Edge: Living with Global Capitalism* (pp. 164–174). London: Cape.

Coleman, L. (2011). Improving Relationship Satisfaction – Qualitative Insights Derived from Individuals Currently within a Couple Relationship. *Family Journal, 19*(4), 369–380.

Coltrane, S. (1996). *Family Man: Fatherhood, Housework and Gender Equity.* New York and Oxford: Oxford University Press.

Doucet, A. (1995). Gender Equality and Gender Difference in Household Work and Parenting. *Women's Studies International Forum, 18*(3), 271–284.

Duncombe, J., & Marsden, D. (1993). Love and Intimacy: The Gender Division of Emotion and 'Emotion Work'. A Neglected Aspect of Sociological Discussion of Heterosexual Relationships. *Sociology, 27*(2), 221–241.

Ernst, E., Rand, J. I., & Stevinson, C. (1998). Complementary Therapies for Depression: An Overview. *Archives of General Psychiatry, 55*(11), 1026–1032.

Finch, J. (1983). *Married to the Job: Wives' Incorporation in Men's Work*. London: Allen and Unwin.

Gabb, J. (2008). *Researching Intimacy in Families*. Basingstoke: Palgrave Macmillan.

Gabb, J. (2013). Embodying Risk: Managing Father–Child Intimacy and the Display of Nudity in Families. *Sociology, 47*(4), 639–654.

Gabb, J., Klett-Davies, M., Fink, J., & Thomae, M. (2013). *Enduring Love? Couple Relationships in the 21st Century. Survey Findings Report*. Milton Keynes: The Open University. Retrieved from http://www.open.ac.uk/researchprojects/enduringlove/files/enduringlove/file/ecms/web-content/Final-Enduring-Love-Survey-Report.pdf.

Giddens, A. (1991). *Modernity and Self-Identity: Self and Society in the Late Modern Age*. Cambridge: Polity Press.

Goldberg, A. E. (2013). 'Doing' and 'Undoing' Gender: The Meaning and Division of Housework in Same-Sex Couples. *Journal of Family Theory and Review, 5*, 85–104.

Heaphy, B., Smart, C., & Einarsdottir, A. (2013). *Same Sex Marriages: New Generations, New Relationships*. Basingstoke: Palgrave Macmillan.

Hochschild, A. R. (1979). Emotion Work, Feeling Rules and Social Structure. *American Journal of Sociology, 85*, 551–575.

Hochschild, A. R. (1989). *The Second Shift: Working Parents and the Revolution at Home*. New York, NY: Viking.

Hochschild, A. R. (2003). *The Commercialization of Intimate Life: Notes from Home and Work*. Berkeley: University of California Press.

Jamieson, L. (1998). *Intimacy: Personal Relationships in Modern Societies*. Cambridge: Polity Press.

Kipnis, L. (1998). Adultery. *Critical Inquiry, 24*(2), 289–327.

Kipnis, L. (2004). *Against Love: A Polemic*. London: Vintage.

Klett-Davies, M., & Skaliotis, E. (2009). Mothers, Childcare and the Work-Life Balance. In S. A. Hunt (Ed.), *Family Trends – British Families Since the 1950s*. London: Family & Parenting Institute.

Langford, W. (1999). *Revolutions of the Heart. Gender, Power and the Delusions of Love*. London: Routledge.

Oakley, A. (2005). *The Ann Oakley Reader*. Bristol: The Policy Press.

ONS. (2012). *Divorces in England and Wales – 2011. Statistical Bulletin*. Retrieved from http://www.ons.gov.uk/ons/dcp171778_291750.pdf

Relationships Alliance. (2013). Focusing on Couples. *The Guardian*, 7 November. Retrieved 29 October 2014, from http://www.theguardian.com/lifeandstyle/2013/nov/07/focusing-couples-relationships

Smart, C. (2007). *Personal Life*. Cambridge: Polity Press.

Szabo, M. (2014). Men Nurturing through Food: Challenging Gender Dichotomies around Domestic Cooking. *Journal of Gender Studies, 23*(1), 18–31.

Walker, J., Barrett, H., Wilson, G., & Chang, Y.-S. (2010). *Understanding the Needs of Adults (Particularly Parents) Regarding Relationship Support. Research Brief DCSF-RBX-10-01*. London: DCFS.

Wetherell, M. (2012). *Affect and Emotion. A New Social Science Understanding*. London: Sage.

Zelizer, V. A. (2005). *The Purchase of Intimacy*. Princeton: Princeton University Press.

3

Communication

In setting out a history of the idea of communication, John Durham Peters (2000) argues that communication has now become a 'registry of modern longings', a term which evokes a 'utopia where nothing is misunderstood, where hearts are open, and expression is uninhibited' (2000, p. 2). Nowhere are these expectations of, and desires for, communication more evident than in contemporary understandings of the couple relationship. We can see the importance of communication as a constant theme in research that informs relationship education and support (Chang & Barrett, 2009) and as a common thread in sociocultural narratives about what makes a 'successful' relationship where, as we noted in Chapters 1 and 2, the influence of popular therapy is ever present (Eldén, 2011; Furedi, 2004). Perhaps not surprisingly, then, given that the couple relationship is always embedded in, and shaped by, wider structures of feeling (Williams, 1977), communication was an important dynamic in the way couples in the *Enduring Love?* study talked about their relationships and explained the everyday practices through which they sustained their lives together. Maintaining good channels of communication with a partner was not necessarily conjoined with proximity. Long-distance communication – mostly in the form of texts and, to a lesser extent, phone calls, emails and letters – was also highly valued

© The Author(s) 2018
J. Gabb, J. Fink, *Couple Relationships in the 21st Century*, Palgrave Macmillan Studies in Family and Intimate Life, DOI 10.1007/978-3-319-59698-3_3

by all couples, resident and non-resident alike. Virtual messages which touched base were often experienced to be as important and meaningful as sharing lengthy conversations together.

Discussion of the significance afforded to communication by couples is organised in this chapter through themes that focus on the importance afforded to talking and listening; establishing intimate knowledge of each other and their relationship; relating to each other as friends; and expressions of love. Interwoven with these themes are considerations of how conflict, as a negative counterpoint to more affirming manifestations of communication, is experienced and managed by couples. This chapter does not, however, extend to the issue of domestic violence (Hanmer & Itzin, 2001; Hearn, 2013) as this fell outside the remit of our study. Our reflections focus on arguments, reflexive bickering and grievances within couple relationships, together with the way that these modes of communication were enacted in interviews.

Talking and listening

Talking and listening offered couples in the *Enduring Love?* study a chance not only to share their experiences inside and outside the home but also to disclose how they felt about an event or issue, in the hope and expectation that their partner would empathise with them. Yet a partner was not simply a conduit through which to unburden oneself after a troublesome day at work or reflect on difficult parenting and childcare issues. It was rather that, in describing practices of talking and listening, couples illustrated the dynamic of good communication in which interchange, mutuality and reciprocity were central (Peters, 2000).

I love talking to my wife and getting her insight

Zoe: [Partner] arrived home soon after 6 and 'debriefed' about some difficult conversations she'd had in the afternoon with project funders. She often does that, and I hope it was helpful – I don't know a lot about the details but try and be a sounding board when she needs to talk something through.

The value placed on such exchanges suggests that couple relationships are one of the few places where women and men believe their voice is heard and where opinions and feelings can be shared and valued. Yet appreciation of this form of communication may also reflect how couples have come to understand their relationships through popular therapeutic discourses, which emphasise the couple relationship as responsible and autonomous and where partners are always there for each other while respecting each other's individuality (Eldén, 2011). Couples' commitment to talking and listening was often driven by a determination to foster intimate knowledge of each other – the 'deep knowing' (Jamieson, 1998) dimension of relationship work which we discussed in Chapter 2 and which is described so pertinently by this young man in his mid-twenties:

ROB: I mean, even if I felt uncomfortable about talking about it, I would talk about it because I said to [partner], no matter how uncomfortable you feel, this is at the beginning of the relationship, or how embarrassing something might be or how bad you feel, we should *always* talk about things. (our emphasis)

Here, communication sets the parameters in establishing Rob's relationship with his partner and its template for the future. The relationship that he is working to build is one that demands constant attention to disclosure. Part of the relationship work that he is undertaking is to encourage his partner to share this mutually disclosing mode of communication. There is then for Rob, and for many other couples in our study, almost a compulsion to talk, again reflecting popular therapeutic discourses that prize openness and dialogue. The couple, as described here, is redolent of Eldén's (2012) 'good couple', comprising two equal partners in constant communication, and the 'pure relationship' invoked by Giddens (1992) – a gender-neutral relationship that is the epitome of agency and capacity. However, for those in couple relationships of a longer duration than Rob's, talking and listening as a mode of communication held different dimensions and meanings.

DEBS: [Partner] came home at 5 to 6 and I served tea at 6. Nice ordinary pleasant family tea. The kids invented the concept of 'interminding' for when you interrupt someone but they don't mind because you read their mind. Thinking about it now, [partner] and I do this a lot to each other – we have conversations that must be completely incomprehensible because sentences and thoughts are not completed and we talk over each other (but are still listening).

For Debs and her partner, the idea of 'interminding' clearly resonates with the modes of communication that they have developed over the years spent together. From the outside, their mutual interruptions could appear dismissive or disrespectful but this abbreviated dialogue is both comprehensible to them and also serves to consolidate their sense of deep knowing. It is their *private* language; they listen to and can hear thoughts unspoken because they know each other so well. In contrast, for Moira, a woman in her late forties, mulling over the minutiae of life is part of the relationship work which consolidates her long-term partnership. Picking over the details of events or everyday shared experiences, both inside and outside the home, is therefore the mode of couple communication which works for this relationship.

MOIRA: We like to go out with each other and ... just get involved in other things and come back and talk. We talk a lot to each other about all sorts of things, about work, about ... We do watch telly occasionally, and just talk about it, you know ... We're interested in what the other might have to say about things. So I think that's really been a cement and a joy.

For both these women, at a midpoint in their life course, conversation is less about unburdening feelings and more about appreciating the way dialogue, in its distinctive *knowing* form, keeps the relationship alive and vibrant.

In distinction to this conversational mode, an unwillingness, inability or reluctance by couples to talk about particular aspects of their life together could result in problematic secrets and silences (Davidoff, Doolittle, Fink, & Holden, 1999; Smart, 2007). Answers to the survey question 'What do you like *least* about your relationship?'[1] reflected how poor communication can be experienced as an unyielding wedge between one partner and the other, or as a source of anxiety. This was particularly the case for women whose answers about the difficulties non-disclosure brings to their relationship were often clustered around the issue of money and an unwillingness of partners to share their feelings.

> Communication about finances – husband is secretive about money and I find it frustrating
> It is very difficult to get my partner to talk about his feelings or about our relationship

In some respects, these gender differences reflect findings from earlier research (Mansfield & Collard, 1988) about 'the phenomena of male non-disclosure and gender asymmetry in emotional behaviour' (Duncombe & Marsden, 1993, p. 229). Yet our qualitative data suggest a more complicated picture of gender differences around emotional intimacy. These data support Brannen and Collard's (1982) contention that disclosure should not always be viewed as a positive dynamic in couples' communication with each other. A more nuanced understanding of how couples communicate shows that there is no one mode that works for everyone. Within these distinctive exchanges gender did, however, remain a crucial factor, although some men's perceived unwillingness to draw painful emotions or stressful events into the realms of what might be talked about with a partner cannot be regarded simply as a product of their 'poor' communication skills. Reluctance to share feelings about 'stressors' can also be understood as an empathetic awareness of the potential impact on the relationship of disclosing one's own emotional frailties and exposing those of one's partner.

GLEN: We've had our ups and downs, we've been having our arguments and stuff like that, but you get over them arguments and discuss it and make up and I don't know [...] I would say losing [our baby] two years ago, we had a still-born and, obviously, me having to support her ... you know, it's been difficult. Obviously the last couple of years have been difficult, emotionally, for me as well ... as well as [partner]. [Partner] wants to have another child and yes, we are going to try again, but a part of me feels that I'm not ready, and part of me feels that I do want to have another child but I'm not [...] because I'm scared. I haven't said this to [partner], but, but that's how I feel. But yeah, we will try again. I just feel that it's too early for us to try and push that while ... the way [partner] is at the moment.

There is evident distress in Glen's account and his heightened emotions are palpable. The loss of their child has left an indelible wound on his relationship, one which he is seeking to heal through silence. His reluctance to talk is not, however, motivated by overriding defensiveness, although it is highly probable that such feelings are present. His decision to conceal his fears of losing another child is also arguably informed by his intimate knowledge of his partner. 'The way she is at the moment' alludes to her depression and it illustrates his understanding that to disclose his reluctance about having another child in the immediate future could be a potential risk to her emotional well-being. His silence is thus his way of deflecting further anxiety away from his partner and shouldering the emotional burden for the couple. In fraught situations and complicated scenarios such as these, keeping silent may be used in an attempt at kindness, a deliberate strategy to protect someone (self and/or partner) from pain and to prevent further distress. Not talking or sharing feelings may, therefore, also be understood as an unspoken investment in the couple rather than an emotional withdrawal from the relationship. As Julie Brownlie (2014) says, research has for too long focused analytical attention on the spoken word; the unsaid is hugely significant. What individuals do and the everyday, ordinary practices that comprise relationships may combine to maintain a sense of shared privacy or constitute a protective shield around one or both partners.

Relating to each other

Couples' intimate knowledge of each other also shapes the extent to which the couple relationship can become a space of personal growth, security and safety – something that was reinforced by the meanings used by couples in our study to describe how they related to each other. Descriptive terms including 'best friend', 'soul mate', 'lover', 'equal partner', 'parent' and 'companion' were widely used, often in multiple combinations. In both survey and qualitative data, the synthesis of different terms was used by participants as a way to articulate their depth of feeling, thus highlighting inadequacies in the terminology that is readily available to describe couple relationships.

We are best friends as well as lovers

SAM: I love her. She is my soul mate. I love being with her [...] She is my best friend. She is intelligent and witty and positive – I love her more than I love myself and I love myself a lot.

In mapping the contours of their relationship, friendship was used repeatedly by couples to signify an emotional closeness which enabled them not only to share concerns and discuss problems but also receive support, advice and understanding. An understanding that friendship between couples could provide a safe arena in which personal traits and shortcomings were not adversely judged also connoted a sense of togetherness and 'being there' for each other (McCarthy, 2012), hence the importance placed on ideas of respect, encouragement and kindness as particularly valued features in their practices of relating. Everyday notions of friendship generally understand it to be a non-sexual relationship and that sexual relationships have a different basis from friendship (Jamieson, 1998). However, our study, like other research in this field (Pahl & Pevalin, 2005), suggests that many couples rarely make such a categorical distinction themselves, something that we explore in more detail in Chapter 5. The sexual and non-sexual dimensions of the couple relationship were perceived as closely intertwined and often afforded equal value, although where friendship became the overarching feature of a relationship, tensions could be identified, with both women and men mourning the loss of the physical and sexual intimacy they had expected to enjoy as a couple.

MONICA: I did go absolutely mad when I said to him, it's just like I feel that we are just not [sighs] ... we're just not a couple; we aren't at the moment; we're just not. We're friends [...] It's not even necessarily about sex or anything, but just sitting there where it's me and him.

The importance placed on friendship in the ways couples described relating to each other was very closely matched by an emphasis on trust. In survey responses to what couples liked best about their relationship,[2] trust, like friendship, was used to embrace a number of practices, feelings and emotions through which couples communicated their care and support for each other. Parenthood was an underlying factor that characterised these responses. Mothers' answers, for example, were particularly focused on 'feeling safe and secure' which, given the nature of our sample, might be linked to an appreciation of being supported by their partners in times of child-rearing and financial vulnerability. More broadly, what survey answers indicated are the ways that partners provide a 'safe haven' for each other, from which the trials, pressures and temptations of the wider world can be kept at bay.

Temptations, notably infidelity, were identified by over 80 per cent of survey participants as something that would break up their relationship, with couples invoking ideas of trust as an implicit signifier of their faithfulness to each other. Questions about the importance of monogamy received almost uniform confirmation; the disclosure of past, present or imagined affairs was perhaps impossible to articulate. Such silences around infidelity may also be driven by other imperatives. As we suggested earlier, and as Esther Perel, cited in Appignanesi (2011, p. 257) has argued so cogently, 'protective opacity' might be preferable to telling truths, and concealment can be a mark of respect for a partner's feelings. The compulsion to disclose and 'tell all' can feign openness when in practice it serves as the confessional through which one party unburdens their guilt onto another as a means to lighten their emotional load.

Online and off-track

British Social Attitudes Survey data highlight the persistent identification of sexual fidelity as crucial to relationship stability (Barlow, Duncan, James, & Park, 2001) and the disclosure or discovery of an affair as the breaking point for around 40 per cent of couples whose relationship has ended (Walker et al., 2010). The impact of affairs on the lives of married couples has thus been the focus of considerable academic attention

(Duncombe, Harrison, Allan, & Marsden, 2004; Lawson, 1988). Recent critical inquiry has expanded the scope of this analysis, focusing on infidelity as an internet phenomenon (Whitty & Quigley, 2008) and suggesting that such experiences are now commonplace and should therefore be perceived as an ordinary part of relationships more than a threat to them (Hakim, 2012). While this latter point lacks empirical evidence to substantiate the claim, there is however a more general acknowledgement that online pornography and sexual–social networking can serve to undermine traditional understandings of intimacy and infidelity in face-to-face relationships (Barker, 2012).

In the *Enduring Love?* study, the use of online pornography was related more to concerns about its threat to the open and transparent ways that couples expected to communicate with each other. Lying about watching pornography online, rather than its actual use, was thus experienced by both partners as deeply problematic because it eroded the importance that couples placed on trust, as this participant explains:

PETER: I don't want to upset her anymore. I do love her so much, like I really, really care and I hate myself for being the way I am … [Partner] says it's more than the actual usage of or watching or downloading, it's more about the lies. But I would lie because I felt ashamed of who I am and what I would do, you know, and I didn't want her to know because I didn't want to jeopardise our love life and our sex life as well and that would really kinda like hurt, that would hurt a lot to me because I knew I was lying to her. But I was lying to her to kinda protect her feelings in a kinda way and also to … so she didn't judge me, I didn't wanna be judged.

Peter sets out here the deep emotional tensions he experiences between the love and care he feels for his partner and the revulsion and shame he feels about himself and his use of online pornography. Lying offers him a way of managing this tension in that it seems to shield his partner from intimate knowledge about who *he* understands himself to be and safeguard their love for each other. At the same time, it also helps him hold at bay fears of being adversely judged. However in seeking to protect himself and his partner's feelings, Peter's deceit transgresses the central premise of mutual disclosure in understandings of the importance of communication for couple relationships. His dishonesty is experienced by his partner as a painful intimation that their relationship is not founded on truth and honesty, thereby undermining her trust in him and the life they have built together. They have begun again, therefore, on their relationship as project, working actively to restore trust by sharing their respective feelings about Peter's use of pornography and the ways they might manage 'the problem' together.

Internet activity encroached in other ways on participant's couple relationships and was experienced as equally unsettling of the connections that were valued and longed for. Managing the boundaries between employment and home, for example, could be difficult when online working was an ever-present and often insistent feature of couples' lives together. When the demands of one partner's work regularly spilt over into the couple's domestic space, the other could be left feeling lonely and neglected.

FIONA: Unfortunately she still had work to do on the computer so we spent the evening in different rooms … and we had spent the whole day either apart or with someone else so I don't feel like we have enough time together. Sometimes she can be so wrapped up in computer stuff that I feel like she forgets I'm in the flat at all.

Others in our study, however, resisted being 'forgotten' and challenged the allure of the internet by creating their own distractions and temptations in order to close down the space it generated in their everyday lives together. Richard's diary entry speaks to his irritation with his partner's reluctance to spend time alone in the evening when he is working on the computer, while recognising at the same time her frustration at not being able to share activities, such as watching TV, with him.

RICHARD: Back home [partner] has cooked – we chat over dinner in dining room – after I need to work on computer upstairs for a chunk of the evening. This is probably our biggest area of friction. I know [partner] doesn't like being left alone while I work on the computer but there's a lot for me to keep up with. [Partner] leaves me to it while she watches TV downstairs. At some point [partner] calls up to ask if I want a cup of tea, and tempts me beyond endurance with choc biscuits. Sometimes she'll call that there's something interesting on the TV.

Both Fiona and Richard illustrate how time spent together apart, when online, can generate conflict and distress if it is not mutually agreed, not least because it is experienced as rejection or exclusion. Yet for other couples, online time was perceived in more positive ways because it created opportunities for both partners to spend time together apart, pursuing personal interests, catching up with friends or enjoying some relaxation time alone. Where constraints in domestic space were particularly acute, as for Zak and his partner, these activities could be a crucial factor in sustaining relationships.

ZAK: We sometimes play video games together or I play a video game on that while she's watching a DVD on that [points to two screens, side by side on desk] … We just, I think, are reminded very much of how much we enjoy ourselves as individuals … Those periods are very special, very important.

For Zak, *being* together and being in a couple relationship are not bounded by physical proximity and mutual intimacy. His online persona and internet activities are multiple and complex. The video games that he and his partner enjoy facilitate closeness and imagined ways of being together, beyond the material. These online activities transport Zak outside of the immediacy of the couple relationship, but he relishes such gaming activities all the more when they take place with his partner sitting beside him. Such living together apart activities, as discussed in Chapter 2, comprise a crucial part of this couple's relationship. They do not need to communicate with each other during these times because their shared pleasure lies in their individual enjoyment of separate activities.

Deep knowing, beyond words

For many couples, their practices of relating to each other were shaped through the intimate knowledge they had of themselves and their partner, thus providing them with a more mediated form of closeness and togetherness than that of friendship. Knowing her partner Russell cognitively and emotionally helps Ella not only identify the reasons why he withdraws at times, but also negotiate the dynamics of their interactions rather than attempt to change or resist them.

ELLA: You don't realise you're doing it, but you're naturally very introvert ... sometimes I leave him and let him have space and then there's other times where it's like, I have to draw him back out again, 'Come back, come back!' [Laughs] And actually when he's like that, he doesn't talk, there's no cuddles, there's no, he does literally just go into himself. But then that's you isn't it, so.

RUSSELL: Yeah, that's another thing ... you've sort of taught me things about myself and I recognise a lot more of what I'm like.

ELLA: That's part of being in a couple I think. It's not just you, it's me as well.

For Ella and her partner, their knowledge of each other is fundamental to 'being in a couple' and to maintaining the intimate connections between them. In their mid-fifties, they met through an online dating site after many years alone following the break-up of their respective marriages. They draw on what they identify as painful and lonely experiences to frame and make sense of their achievement of this level of insight about themselves and how they have acquired the knowledge necessary to sustain *this* couple relationship. For other couples, however, where only one partner drew on an intimate knowledge of the other, the emotional registers around relating to each other were much more fluid. Here, Leona explains the pain and pathos of her partner's failure to comfort her following her father's funeral, while holding on to what she understood to be his absurd behaviour.

LEONA: I had tears streaming down my face and I was obviously in a bit of a mess and he ... he looked across to the garage as we went past, he pulled in and said, 'I'm just gonna go and have a quick look' [laughter]. And he got out of the car and left me in the car and went and had a look at the BMW and the Mercedes and the [laughter] cars that were over there and then got back in [higher pitch] and carried on driving [...] I was mad with him but I just couldn't get anything out [laughter] [...] He didn't see anything wrong with doing that [...] that's just because of the way he handles it opposed to the way that I handle it.

Leona's reflexive account of this scenario indicates that she did not perceive her partner's behaviour as simply uncaring or thoughtless. Instead she drew on her knowledge and understanding of their respective ways of managing stressful situations to explain his actions and his inability to see 'anything wrong' in what he had done. For some couples this would be an unacceptable way of relating to each other but for Leona, it allowed her to accommodate – albeit with equal measures of dismay and humour – the gender asymmetry that marked the different configurations of emotional behaviour in their relationship.

Yet a capacity for understanding a partner's behaviour or an ability to reflect on one's own way of being was not always sufficient to reconcile differences. Survey responses indicated that 'certain patterns of behaviour' become engrained in couple relationships and, in turn, provoke arguments that cannot be deflected. This is replicated in our qualitative data, too, where couples showed a clear awareness of how one partner's behaviour prompted a particular way of relating that invariably generated quarrels. Here, for example, one participant bemoaned her own repeated failures to acknowledge the support and care offered by her partner:

RUTH: I just do something really, bloody thoughtless, like that [...] he'll do the shopping and cook a nice meal and I'll go, 'God, these veggies are a bit cold!' [Makes gunshot sound, laughs)] [...] So we row about, about that.

While another participant illustrated how her temper regularly generated conflict in her relationship:

FIONA: Had a bit of a row this evening. Our brand new wok is broken after I burnt dinner in it last week. I can get angry very quickly if I feel like I'm being accused of something even if I know it's my fault. Because of this I can become quite snappy and irritable … We kissed a little after the row which always calms me down. I went out to get a replacement dinner plus some biscuits as an apology to her for losing my temper.

Such patterns in the conflicts experienced in couple relationships cannot be easily mapped onto one or more of our analytic axes of gender, parenting and generation, although as we discuss later in the chapter, housework and childcare were a particular feature of disputes in the study. Sexual orientation was similarly absent as a factor in differentiating modes of couple communication. Couples readily acknowledged a capacity for defensiveness or thoughtlessness, often imbuing its recounting with a sense of regret, amusement and resignation. To avoid any escalation in conflict between them, couples thus opted to 'work things out'; 'agree to differ'; or 'try to ignore it'. However, *knowing* that one's ways of relating to a partner could provoke conflict rarely seemed to minimise its impact or reduce its incidence.

Differences, arguments and reflexive bickering

The arguments and conflict that can result from difficulties in the ways couples relate to each other was ranked in our survey answers as the issue fathers and men without children liked *least* overall about their relationship.[3] Women's responses placed it second overall. Yet differences in each other's views, attitudes and opinions, and the disagreements that they generated, were also understood as a potentially positive feature by some in that they could strengthen a relationship and a couple's capacity to communicate. This was not the case with regard to domestic chores and childcare, where different expectations around taking responsibility for this aspect of the couple relationship appeared to generate much more intractable grievances. Indeed, survey answers typically *combined* inequalities in the sharing of childcare and housework as a source of irritation and conflict, thus reflecting wider debates and research around the effects of a gendered division of labour within the home for couple relationships (Kornich, Brines, & Leupp, 2013; Ruppanner, 2012; Schober, 2013).

> Unequal share of housework and children stuff – no matter how many hints I drop
> The relationship is really one-sided. I work, look after the kids and do all the housework, etc.

Money problems were also cited equally by women and men as an issue they liked least about their relationship, although perhaps counter-intuitively, fathers' answers suggested that they regarded money as significantly less of a problem in their relationship than men without children. However, disputes around money were often dismissed by unemployed couples living on meagre budgets who, like Noel and Jennie, spoke with pride about the way they successfully managed their financial resources together.

JENNIE: […] money I love it, we just don't have enough of it. […]
NOEL: All of the Jobseeker's goes into hers and then when everything's been paid for we just split whatever's left. […]
JENNIE: If bills have to be paid, I get on with it don't I?
NOEL: Yeah. I mean, like Jennie said, the bills are priority you know?
JENNIE: And putting food and clothes on the kids comes before anything we need, so, no, we never argue about money. If we've got extra we've got extra, great we'll do something. If we haven't, it's tough luck, get on with it. No, we never argue about money.

As this exchange also indicates, unemployment is not experienced by Noel as a threat to his masculine identity, a finding reinforced in his individual interview where he talked about a willingness to become a 'house husband' if his partner found work before him. For other men, however, unemployment and being supported financially by a partner could be a deeply stressful time as well as a source of frustration and discord within their relationship.

THEO: When I was unemployed and [partner] was earning it became a stressor, not in the sense that I was asking for money or whatever [...] but that I was constantly striving to reduce the monetary footprint I was causing [...] I was at home all day but I was knocking the electric off at the mains so I couldn't use the computer or television and I was sleeping late deliberately to get to the evening when the heating was cheaper and I was leaving the house to go to places [...] so I wasn't costing money [...] I felt weak and useless for not contributing so I was constantly trying to reduce my burden on [partner].

Possible explanations of these different responses to the experience of male unemployment and its impact on the couple relationship bring into view the importance of attending to couple diversity. Although Noel and Theo are very similar in age and had equally disadvantaged childhoods, Theo has undergraduate and postgraduate degrees while Noel has only minimal educational qualifications. Theo's partner has a similar educational background to him and is, as they both acknowledged, from an affluent middle-class family. Noel's partner's educational and family background reflects his. Being unable to find work undermined Theo's perception of himself as an upwardly mobile young man and threatened his status as economic provider for his middle-class wife (Britt & Huston, 2012). However, Noel, who was long-term unemployed and in poor health, physically and mentally, had few social or cultural resources; his sense of self was given meaning through the relationship work he did as partner and father, in the home, rather than his potential status as an employed man in the wider public sphere. This may have been because couples like Noel and Jennie experience society more as a threat and, therefore, view the family as a refuge (Bawin-Legros, 2004). Attending to these differently classed and gendered dimensions of their respective relationships as well as the ways in which these dimensions were shaped by the social mobility often offered by education, is therefore important.

It offers a valuable example of how the socio-economic contexts in which couple relationships are lived might limit or open up possible terrains of conflict between partners. It also highlights how researchers may need to refocus the methodological lens to include differences and the specificities of context, such as class.

As Les Back (2007) reminds us, working-class lives are often characterised as expressionless and lacking in both sensitivity and commitment. This, he argues, is a consequence of middle-class researcher-bias more than a true representation of the lives and loves among working class communities, wherein forms of communication and displays of affection are not epitomised by the compulsion to disclose our every feeling (Giddens, 1992):

> Love is given a name: it is incarnate. But this commitment is not made in elaborated speeches. It is performed rather than described. It is a kind of illocutionary love, a love that is expressed without painstaking announcement. (Back, 2007, p. 82)

While couple interviews with Noel and Theo and their respective partners pointed to the issues about which couples might (or might not) argue, the *process* of interviewing couples together offered us an equally valuable lens through which to explore questions of conflict and the ways in which they were managed.[4] How couples told stories together about their relationships thus provided us with a further opportunity to extend our understandings of 'the dynamics (socio-cultural, interpersonal and power) that shape the scripting and doing of relationships in practice' (Heaphy & Einarsdottir, 2013, p. 54).

Discussions of collages in the couple interviews in the *Enduring Love?* study were led by the researcher but the couple had to manage, together, their engagements with the questions that were posed. Some couples listened attentively to each other, expanded on the detail of experiences being recounted or carefully explained how and why their views and opinions might differ from those of their partners. For others, the interview was made up of the briefest of 'rallies' around each collage. This meant – pushing the tennis analogy further – that one partner would bat their thoughts on an issue to the other, whereupon it was immediately volleyed back with confirmation of, or challenge to, the viewpoint being expressed. At other times, these interactions can only be described as reflexive bickering. Couples simultaneously joked with and criticised each other as they wove accounts of their lives together into discussion of the collages. As a mode of communication, between the couple and in interaction with the researcher, such bickering was often marked by one partner's ridiculing of, for example, the other's behaviour at a particular moment in their relationship and mock indignation or bewilderment at such reproaches on the part of the other. Laughter overlaid the sparring positions taken up by both partners but point scoring could be equally present, illustrating how couples' ways of communicating with each other can be situated at multiple points in the continuum between criticism and praise, acceptance and disapproval. These interactions also revealed much about the way specific experiences generated discord and dissent, enabling us to identify and examine the extent to which conflicts around particular issues in the past become irresolvable features of the relationship in the present and the future. 'Not this old chestnut!' Frances complained when her partner talked about the misunderstandings around the 'messy start' to their relationship.

Laughter, humour and banter

While couple interviews demonstrated the traces and patterns of conflict and poor communication in relationships, they also illustrated the enormous pleasure of effective couple communication, particularly where laughter was involved. The pleasure and enjoyment that could be experienced in long-term relationships was a recurring theme in our survey where women's answers ranked 'laughing together' as the *best liked* items overall of their relationship with their partner.[5]

> We laugh a lot and bring out the best in each other
> We laugh at ourselves and each other

Both mothers and childfree women appreciated the ways in which they could have a 'good laugh' with their partner, thus strengthening the bonds between them and alleviating the strains and difficulties of every-day life (Barelds & Barelds-Dijkstra, 2010). Having a laugh can thus be seen as a sign of being close, but laughter and banter were also an impor-tant element of the ways in which participants reminisced together about particular incidents in their relationship histories. The humour of these co-narrations was reinforced by the roles adopted by the couples in their 'Goffmanian team performance' during their interviews (Norrick, 2004). So, for example, banter was an integral part of the way Tony and Sophie performed the story of his marriage proposal to her.

TONY: I always feel for people who get engaged on a beach in the Caribbean because how often are you going to be able to go back there and reminisce about it?

SOPHIE: Yeah! [Laughs]. But we can always go back to windy Wales. How many times have you been on Facebook and someone's 'in New York' … or Paris? So I'm glad you didn't do anything like that, because I'd just find that really cheesy […]

TONY: I bet you're so glad I didn't take you to New York! [Laughter]. I can't think of anything worse!

SOPHIE: But as a story, it's a good story in comparison to some of my friends, or just going to a restaurant.

TONY: Yeah, I'm glad it's something I'll never have to do again.

SOPHIE: Why? Did you think I'd say, 'No' and push you over the aqueduct?

TONY: Oh no, I knew you'd be a 'Yes'.

SOPHIE: Oh really!!!? [Laughing hard].

The lively playfulness of banter is used by this couple to unfold their 'engagement story' and present their relationship as one which resists romantic cultural norms often associated with marriage proposals, such as exotic backdrops. However, at the same time, their 'team performance' uses humour to simultaneously reinforce and disrupt normative gender roles that shape assumptions about the ways in which marriage proposals are performed. On the one hand, the time and location of the proposal in this story had been decided by Tony without his partner's knowledge, thereby reducing her to a less than equal partner in the relationship

(Eldén, 2012). On the other hand, Sophie's pleasure in the decisions taken by Tony and the way in which she presents her account of the proposal suggest that banter and humour are being used not only to reinforce their sense of togetherness but also to display that attachment to others. Tony and Sophie therefore used the couple interview as a vehicle through which to 'display' their relationship (Finch, 2007) and the ways they relate to each other, themes that we return to in Chapter 5.

The relations of love and loving relations

The final strand in this chapter is focused on love. In western cultures, romantic love is often presumed to be the driver in relationship formations, and companionate love the bond that holds relationships in place in the longer term since romantic love cannot be sustained in enduring relationships (Acevedo & Aron, 2009). There were, however, no such easy distinctions made by couples in the *Enduring Love?* study. In survey answers and our qualitative data, romantic and companionate love appeared to have very leaky boundaries with couples talking in diverse and slippery ways about how love was expressed and experienced in their relationship. Our discussion here thus reflects Carol Smart's argument that love is 'something that one "does" and "feels" with others rather than a pre-existing type of emotion that one "has"' (Smart, 2007, p. 59).

Feelings of 'being in love and/or being loved' were not highly rated in what women and men in our survey liked *best* about their relationship although attention to gender and the absence/presence of children reveal some interesting differences.[6] Mothers' answers rated 'being in love and/or being loved' most highly but also often made connections in their answers between their children and the feelings of love they shared with their partner.

> Love and our little boy
> We love our children

This dynamic of love is powerfully illustrated in one of the collages (Figure 3.1) produced as part of the participatory research with socially

Figure 3.1 The multiple meanings of love

disadvantaged communities.[7] The collage was designed by Maddie, a married woman in her early thirties, using materials from a range of weekly and monthly magazines targeted at female readers. Maddie has two children under five and although her partner is employed, they have few financial resources and would be defined in contemporary policy terms as 'working poor', that is, working people with incomes below the poverty line (Shildrick, MacDonald, Webster, & Garthwaite, 2012). While producing the collage, she talked at length about how much she loved her partner and their hopes for the future.

At the very heart (literally and metaphorically) of Maddie's collage is a widely reproduced image of an intimately entwined couple who capture, for her, the charm and allure of the romantic relationship. Around this are clippings referring to her husband as sexual partner and soul mate together with other cuttings pointing to notions of companionate love as a site of togetherness and friendship and for sharing difficulties and problems. We can also trace the love she feels for her children and her home. As a whole, then, the collage helps to demonstrate how 'being in love' for mothers might resist not only any easy dichotomy between romantic and companionate love but also, as Chapter 5 argues, the overarching centrality of the couple dyad in their relationships.

Survey responses by women without children were equally complex. These ranked 'being in love and/or being loved' lower than those of mothers, fathers and men without children but their answers rated a partner's 'saying or showing love' the most highly in what made them feel appreciated.[8] This suggests that discourses of love, romance and coupledom (Pearce, 2007; Swidler, 2003) might have different resonances for couples with and without children and that love might also be differently 'felt' and 'done'. However, saying and showing love was an important element in the ways in which all couples communicated with each other. Words, acts and gestures that showed love brought a reassuring sense of closeness and togetherness. When articulated as a question – 'Do you love me?' – one partner's feelings of vulnerability and anxiety could be demonstrated to the other and assuaged by a positive response. Where such expressions disappeared from a relationship completely, they were sorely missed and couples struggled to understand and accommodate the change:

> We don't express our love to each other anymore, it feels weird

Nevertheless, what couples meant when they said 'I love you' to each other was far from straightforward and was seldom associated with a simple verbal expression of love. Just saying 'I love you' was singled out by some participants in our study as not enough in and of itself; it was belief in the meaning and sincerity of these sentiments that was valued alongside demonstrations that 'proved' the integrity of these sentiments.

> Saying I love you and meaning it
> Tells me she loves me and always puts me first

Saying 'I love you' is thus a form of the relationship work we described in Chapter 2: an act of love through which to implicitly communicate apologies, thanks, regrets and goodbyes, convey acceptance of a partner for who s/he is, or diffuse stress and tension. Saying and hearing 'I love you' in tense situations could be enormously effective in managing potential conflict within the home, as this diary extract illustrates:

DEBS: [Partner] went off to put the kids to bed while I cleared up tea (we usually do it like this – whoever's seen least of the kids puts them to bed). I heard [partner] shouting quite a lot. Then I heard him shouting in a way that I find quite scary. I started heading upstairs and he shouted again in the same way. Both kids were sat on the loo sobbing, but then changing in a flash to messing around and laughing [...] a familiar routine where the subtext between the adults was 'one of the adults is at the end of their tether and is behaving badly and really needs a break' rather than a blaming kind of taking over. At some point I caught [partner]'s eye and mouthed 'I love you' to him. He mouthed 'I love you' back to me.

For Debs and her partner, saying 'I love you' on this occasion was layered with multiple meanings and different imperatives. It provided reassurance, putting the fraught and upsetting situation in context. Children's bedtime was often a bittersweet experience for parenting couples in our study. The moment was cherished as important parent–child time but also sometimes resented as it drew energy from already spent resources and ate into evening couple time when adult company and partner intimacy might be enjoyed. Debs' timely intervention of 'I love you' thus served to both calm the situation and reconnect the couple through their shared endeavour as working parents of young children.

It is important, though, not to lose sight of the *cultural specificity* of verbal articulations of love, so too the ways this shapes expectations of how love is communicated and experienced in couple relationships. Some couples from minority ethnic backgrounds explained how rarely they said 'I love you', instead expressing their love through 'all kinds of things'. For example, Georgina and Anton, a Kenyan couple, explain here what they mean by such 'things':

GEORGINA: [He] helps a lot in the house. That's a way of saying I love you, I feel. You know, he helps with the house chores [...] he hoovers and does the dishes. [...]

ANTON: [Love] is routinised in most African marriages [...] it's fulfilled in the relationship, and it's not verbalised [...] You can

> say anything but you're not meaning it. I think that's what's
> happening in the western world.

Being attentive to the specificity of relationship experience is crucial if
couple diversity is to be included in policy-making and if research is to
embed the breadth of couple experience in studies of intimate life (Gabb
& Singh, 2014). Western love, as characterised in the popular imaginary,
has a particular teleology; it has its roots in twelfth-century France where
the Provençal poets 'offered an image and ideal of courtly love worthy of
imitation' (Featherstone, 1999, p. 2). The 'sexualisation of love' emerged
in nineteenth-century discourses on marriage, only becoming fully
fledged in the new 'intimate culture' of the twentieth century. It was only
at this point in time that sexual attraction became associated with love
and sexual relations became a means of solidifying socially acceptable
matches (Seidman, 1991). Love, in this western context, remains irrevocably and unequally gendered (Illouz, 2012) and across our study this
gendered dimension typically shaped women and men's ways of showing
and verbally expressing love. While by no means exclusively, men were far
more likely to show love through everyday acts and gestures rather than
regularly saying 'I love you'.

GARETH: [Partner] tells me she loves me all the time and I don't say, 'I
           love you' as much. I do say it but I don't say it anywhere near
           as much as she does, because I like to try and show her. I like
           to try and do things.

However, as the extract from Gareth illustrates, men's reticence or dis-
inclination to say 'I love you' did not *mean* anything in terms of the
depth of feeling experienced or its perceived centrality in their lives.
Acts and gestures were perceived as deeply personal and fondly cherished by couples. Emma's account of her partner's cooking suggests that
women recognised and valued such acts as one of the many lexicons
of love. Being able to appreciate such unspoken feelings comprised an
important part of couple's intimate knowledge, an understanding that
developed over time.

EMMA: I really, really appreciate it when he does the cooking for me
            and you know he always says, 'Oh I put lots of love into it'
            or you know, he's prepared it with love. And so ... I guess
            him cooking for me is kind of an act of love.

In the survey, acts and gestures that were mentioned as articulations of
love included cooking, making cups of tea, sharing household chores and
childcare and making a partner laugh – all forms of everyday relationship
work that we discussed earlier. Yet by turning the analytic lens of love
onto these mundane activities, it is also possible to understand how they
evoke feelings of love and thus enrich and sustain the emotional connections between couples in very particular ways.

MONA: Told [partner] about [friend's] 'risqué' stories and she
            laughed. I love it when [she] laughs – it makes my heart float
            right out of my chest and bob about.
JEMMA: [Partner] had left me a tea cup with a teabag, some chocolate
            and a lovely note. This all made me smile, I love [partner] so
            much.

These private repertoires of love bring together all the different dimensions of communication that have been explored in this chapter and illustrate how couples relate to each other through practices and feelings that
are testimony of the depth and breadth of their lives together. Talking and
listening to each other lays down and maintains the foundations of their
lives together and opens up new possibilities for the relationship in the
future. Intimate knowledge is used by couples to communicate their love
through words and deeds that are special, private and personally meaningful to them. However, as we have also suggested, words and deeds
can be equally riven with anger, frustration and distress. The negative
and positive emotions that fuel communication between couples are thus
ever present, and some of the most difficult relationship work engaged in
by couples is in negotiating the boundaries between potentially destructive conflicts and constructive forms of communication. Findings from
the *Enduring Love?* study suggest that where management of differences

and disagreements succeeds, this can become another deeply meaningful dimension of the relationship.

Notes

1. See Appendix 2, Table A2.3: 'What do you like least about your relationship?'
2. See Appendix 2, Table A2.2: 'What do you like best about your relationship?'
3. See Appendix 2, Table A2.3: 'What do you like least about your relationship?'
4. See Appendix 1 for discussion of this method.
5. See Appendix 2, Table A2.2: 'What do you like best about your relationship?'
6. See Appendix 2, Table A2.2: 'What do you like best about your relationship?'
7. See Appendix 1 for more details about this part of our study.
8. See Appendix 2, Table A2.1: 'What does your partner do for you that makes you feel appreciated?'

References

Acevedo, B. P., & Aron, A. (2009). Does a Long-Term Relationship Kill Romantic Love? *Review of General Psychology, 13*(1), 59–65.

Appignanesi, L. (2011). *All About Love: Anatomy of an Unruly Emotion*. London: Virago Press.

Back, L. (2007). *The Art of Listening*. Oxford and New York: Berg.

Barelds, D. P. H., & Barelds-Dijkstra, P. (2010). Humor in Intimate Relationships: Ties Among Sense of Humor, Similarity in Humor and Relationship Quality. *Humor, 23*(4), 447–465.

Barker, M. (2012). *Rewriting the Rules*. London: Routledge.

Barlow, A., Duncan, S., James, G., & Park, A. (2001). *Just a Piece of Paper? Marriage and Cohabitation. British Social Attitudes: The 18th Report: Public Policy, Social Ties*. London: Sage.

Bawin-Legros, B. (2004). Intimacy and the New Sentimental Order. *Current Sociology, 52*(2), 241–250.

Brannen, J., & Collard, J. (1982). *Marriages in Trouble: The Process of Seeking Help*. London: Tavistock.

Britt, S. L., & Huston, S. J. (2012). The Role of Money Arguments in Marriage. *Journal of Family and Economic Issues, 33*(4), 464–476.

Brownlie, J. (2014). *Ordinary Relationships: A Sociological Study of Emotions, Reflexivity and Culture*. Basingstoke: Palgrave Macmillan.

Chang, Y.-S., & Barrett, H. (2009). *Couple Relationships: A Review of the Nature and Effectiveness of Support Services*. London: Family and Parenting Institute.

Davidoff, L., Doolittle, M., Fink, J., & Holden, K. (1999). *The Family Story: Blood, Contract and Intimacy, 1830–1960*. London: Longman.

Duncombe, J., Harrison, K., Allan, G., & Marsden, D. (2004). *The State of Affairs: Explorations in Infidelity and Commitment*. London: Routledge.

Duncombe, J., & Marsden, D. (1993). Love and Intimacy: The Gender Division of Emotion and 'Emotion Work'. A Neglected Aspect of Sociological Discussion of Heterosexual Relationships. *Sociology, 27*(2), 221–241.

Eldén, S. (2011). The Threat or Promise of Popular Therapy? A Feminist Reading of Narratives of 'The Good Couple'. *NORA – Nordic Journal of Feminist Research, 19*(3), 144–162.

Eldén, S. (2012). Scripts for the 'Good Couple': Individualization and the Reproduction of Gender Inequality. *Acta Sociologica, 55*(1), 3–18.

Featherstone, M. (1999). *Love & Eroticism*. London: Sage.

Finch, J. (2007). Displaying Families. *Sociology, 41*(1), 65–81.

Furedi, F. (2004). *Therapy Culture: Cultivating Vulnerability in an Uncertain Age*. London: Routledge.

Gabb, J., & Singh, R. (2014). Reflections on the Challenges of Understanding Racial, Cultural and Sexual Differences in Couple Relationship Research. *Journal of Family Therapy*. doi:10.1111/1467-6427.12044.

Giddens, A. (1992). *The Transformation of Intimacy: Sexuality, Love and Eroticism in Modern Societies*. Cambridge: Polity Press.

Hakim, C. (2012). *The New Rules: Internet Dating, Playfairs and Erotic Power*. London: Gibson Square Books.

Hanmer, J., & Itzin, C. (Eds.). (2001). *Home Truths About Domestic Violence: Feminist Influences on Policy and Practice*. London: Routledge.

Heaphy, B., & Einarsdottir, A. (2013). Scripting Civil Partnerships: Interviewing Couples Together and Apart. *Qualitative Research, 13*(1), 53–70.

Hearn, J. (2013). The Sociological Significance of Domestic Violence: Tensions, Paradoxes and Implications. *Current Sociology, 61*(2), 152–170.

Illouz, E. (2012). *Why Love Hurts*. Cambridge: Polity Press.

Jamieson, L. (1998). *Intimacy: Personal Relationships in Modern Societies.* Cambridge: Polity Press.

Kornich, S., Brines, J., & Leupp, K. (2013). Egalitarianism, Housework and Sexual Frequency in Marriage. *American Sociological Review, 78*(1), 26–50.

Lawson, A. (1988). *Adultery.* London: Basic Books.

Mansfield, P., & Collard, J. (1988). *The Beginning of the Rest of Your Life?* London: Macmillan.

McCarthy, J. R. (2012). The Powerful Relational Language of 'Family': Togetherness, Belonging and Personhood. *Sociological Review, 60*(1), 68–90.

Norrick, N. R. (2004). Humor, Tellability, and Conarration in Conversational Storytelling. *Text, 24*(1), 79–111.

Pahl, R., & Pevalin, D. (2005). Between Family and Friends: A Longitudinal Study of Friendship Choice. *British Journal of Sociology, 56*(3), 433–450.

Pearce, L. (2007). *Romance Writing.* Cambridge: Polity Press.

Peters, J. D. (2000). *Speaking into the Air: A History of the Idea of Communication.* Chicago: Chicago University Press.

Ruppanner, L. (2012). Housework, Conflict and Divorce: A Multi-Level Analysis. *Work, Employment and Society, 26*(4), 638–656.

Schober, P. S. (2013). The Parenthood Effect on Gender Inequality: Explaining the Change in Paid and Domestic Work When British Couples Become Parents. *European Sociological Review, 29*(1), 74–85.

Seidman, S. (1991). *Romantic Longings: Love in America 1830–1980.* London: Routledge.

Shildrick, T., MacDonald, R., Webster, C., & Garthwaite, K. (2012). *Poverty and Insecurity: Life in Low-Pay, No-Pay Britain.* Bristol: Policy Press.

Smart, C. (2007). *Personal Life.* Cambridge: Polity Press.

Swidler, A. (2003). *Talk of Love: How Culture Matters.* Chicago: Chicago University Press.

Walker, J., Barrett, H., Wilson, G., & Chang, Y.-S. (2010). *Understanding the Needs of Adults (Particularly Parents) Regarding Relationship Support. Research Brief DCSF-RBX-10-01.* London: DCFS.

Whitty, M., & Quigley, L. L. (2008). Emotional and Sexual Infidelity Offline and in Cyberspace. *Journal of Marital and Family Therapy, 34*(4), 461–468.

Williams, R. (1977). *Marxism and Literature.* Oxford: Oxford University Press.

4

Sex and Intimacy

There is a wealth of research on sex and sexual intimacy which builds on and extends the pioneering sex survey research of Kinsey et al. (1948, 1953) and the sociological studies of Masters and Johnson (1966, 1970). Findings from the most recent wave of the Natsal survey provide fresh insight on sexual behaviour, attitudes, health and well-being across the UK population, highlighting the progressive liberalisation of sexual attitudes and lifestyles (Natsal, 2013). Analysis which falls under the broadly defined sociological umbrella has sought to problematise sex by situating sex and sexuality in context. Work in this vein has drawn attention to the ways that sexual scripts shape sexuality and gendered sex lives (e.g., Johnson, 2005; Kimmel, 2007; Plummer, 1995; Simon & Gagnon, 2003 Building on early).second-wave feminist work on the political meanings of sex (Koedt, 1973; Rich, 1980), this body of work has also usefully focused attention on heterosexuality as a site of gendered norms, sex and power (Hockey et al., 2010; Jackson, 1999; Langford, 1999; Meadows, 1997; Rahman & Jackson, 2010). Studies of same-sex relationships have similarly highlighted the intersections of sexuality and power and the ways that understandings of sex lives and sexual identities are constituted through socio-cultural and historical domains (Plummer, 1995) wherein public–private worlds intersect to shape contemporary intimate

© The Author(s) 2018
J. Gabb, J. Fink, *Couple Relationships in the 21st Century*, Palgrave Macmillan Studies
in Family and Intimate Life, DOI 10.1007/978-3-319-59698-3_4

life (Berlant, 1997; Frank, Clough, & Seidman, 2013). In this work, sex has been troubled as a site of desire, longing and despair (Berlant & Edelman, 2013), with queer studies focusing critical attention on the contested meanings of sex beyond the heteronorm (Frye, 1991; Stein, 1997; Wilton, 1996). Research on bisexuality has further extended these analyses by calling into question the underpinning binary of 'the sexes' (Barker & Langdridge, 2008). This rich and wide-ranging body of work reminds us that, while sex may be an important means of intimate expression and a source of sustainable pleasure for some people, for others it can be an uncomfortable and sometimes emotionally painful area of personal life (Smart, 2007).

We situate our analysis of sexual intimacy in the context of these studies and critical inquiry. Like other findings presented thus far, the experience of sexual intimacy in the *Enduring Love?* study was not defined through types of relationship but instead criss-crossed the sexual spectrum. However, sexual experience was significantly shaped by a range of factors including age, parenting status, gender and biography – perhaps more so than most other forms of relationship practice. In many ways, as Chapter 3 discussed, how love and intimacy were experienced, understood and deployed in couple relationships drifted in and out of focus across couples' accounts of their intimate lives together, sometimes being situated at the forefront of what was said and at other times being left unarticulated or hinted at in ambiguous terms. Yet intimacy and togetherness remained the underlying context. Sex was typically embedded within emotional dimensions of the relationship rather than seen as a simply physical encounter.

Engendering intimacy

In response to the survey question, 'What does your partner do for you that makes you feel appreciated?',[1] answers included under the rubric of 'physical affection' ranged from fleeting gestures to tender moments of intimacy. Our analysis thus focuses on the range and meanings of intimate experience and the temporal dimensions of such relationship practices. Indeed, time and the quotidian rhythms of a relationship were perceived as crucial features in nurturing and nourishing a partnership. Many of the answers either explicitly stated or implicitly implied that it was the regularity of intimate contact that was appreciated alongside the gesture itself.

> Greets me with a kiss every evening when I come in from work
> Strokes my hair until I sleep
> Rubs my back every night

A kiss, caress and massage were all frequently mentioned by participants and included here in coded responses as physical affection. These *touching* gestures appear to be experienced as a sign of their partner's appreciation both because of the thoughtfulness of the gesture and because of its corresponding mutuality. That is to say, a tactile gesture can never be singular because when we touch something we are automatically touched back (Gabb, 2011). Couples emotionally and symbolically connect through these reciprocal interactions; such embodied sensations of touch fold us back upon ourselves and produce a reflexive response (Grosz, 1993). The touching caress of a partner therefore serves to connect the couple *in relation* to each other.

Gender was not a distinguishing variable for these survey responses; indeed, there was marked congruence between the answers of women and men, with both groups appearing to equally and highly appreciate physical affection. The answers of mothers and fathers were equally aligned, although for this group their answers ranked it less highly than other things identified. Survey data thus portrayed a gender-neutral picture of physical affection. In the study's qualitative data, however, evident gendered differences could be identified and in many cases these did appear to shape the couple dynamic. These differences between qualitative interview and survey data should not, however, be read as epistemological contradiction (Hesse-Biber, 2010); instead, they point to the tensions between reported relationship ideals (what couples *should* do) and rich accounts of lived experience (the messiness of what couples do *in practice*). As such, the disparity between these data adds further gravitas to the meaningfulness of physical affection in the couple relationship as couples wrestle with the relationships they live with and those they live by (Gillis, 1996).

Lucy and Garry, for example, openly acknowledged their different levels of need for hugs and physical affection, situating this within the context of their particular relationship narrative.

LUCY: I probably crave more hugging type affection than you do, would you say that's true?

GARRY: Yeah.

LUCY: But I've got used to not getting it …

GARRY: We, kind of, gravitate to different positions [on individual sofas] but it's not by design, is it? Although, when there's been a swap over very occasionally, the remark will be made, 'Don't get too comfortable on my sofa.' But that's just –

LUCY: All very tongue-in-cheek.

GARRY: Laughing and joking, you know. I think you want cuddles more than me.

LUCY: I do like a cuddle and I would like Garry to say, 'Oh, come over here and have a cuddle,' very occasionally. And sometimes I have told you that, haven't I? There are times when I do crave more –

GARRY: Contact.

The exchange in this interview is telling on many levels, demonstrating how Lucy and Garry negotiate difficult areas of their relationship through good-humoured banter – a communication strategy that was deployed by many couples in the study, as discussed in Chapter 3. Here, we can see how the couple interview brought together the otherwise 'his' and 'hers' format of individual interviews and facilitated insight into how couples relate to each other (Heaphy & Einarsdottir, 2013). For Lucy and Garry, it enabled them to build a combined account of physical affection that accommodates both 'the issue' and Garry's acknowledgement of his partner's need for greater physical intimacy. The relationship they portray demonstrates a marked difference between the two parties and is quite traditionally gendered. In the following couple interview with Alun and Eleri, gender appears to be decentred as the differentiating feature in their couple relationship, but its salience nevertheless remains between the lines.

ALUM: Intimacy. We're quite tactile, aren't we? We're quite huggy, kissy and touchy and feely.

ELERI: Yeah, I remember after the last interview … it got me thinking about it a little bit more in the interview. And I realised that we did things like, sometimes we brush our teeth together and we hold hands brushing our teeth! [High pitched] I hadn't noticed it and I was just, like, this is ridiculous. Holding hands! A, it's impractical; we've got a tiny bathroom and we have to shove each other out the way to spit when we are brushing our teeth. But I hadn't … I don't think I'd really noticed.

ALUM: Well, I hadn't until you mentioned it and I wouldn't … I don't think I would have noticed it otherwise.

ELERI: No. So, whenever we're in here watching telly, we're connected physically in some way.

Both Alun and Eleri talked fondly about the physical closeness of their relationship, an embodied proximity which facilitates couple connection. This heterosexual couple clearly cherish physical contact equally and openly talked about their 'touchy feely' predispositions. It is interesting to note, however, that it is the female partner who noticed the affection which accompanied their bathroom rituals *and* ascribed meaning to this interaction – something that was otherwise unnoticed by her partner. This greater attentiveness to the couple and how they physically and emotionally interact was mirrored in other couples' data although emotional investment and physical affection were not the exclusive purview of women. Many men were keen to highlight their openly expressive and tactile nature.

RODNEY: I think it's in my nature. I'm, kind of, a tactile person, you know? … My father was a lot like that. I think I have that from my father … and [partner's] family also is very huggy … we both come from families where you express affection, physically, by, you know, big hugs and holding hands and stuff like that, yeah.

In many accounts of couple intimacy, participants sought to explain and justify why they behaved the way they did, both looking inwards at the couple dynamic and outwards at their relational biography (Heaphy et al., 2013), with behaviour being traced back and forth across their past, present and intimate futures. The desire to locate behaviour was sometimes defensive, driven by a compulsion to rationalise what might otherwise be perceived as an omission or 'personal failing'. But on many occasions, as with Rodney, it was used to embed a sense of togetherness through invocation of a unified stance – articulated through, and enshrined in, the combined pronoun 'we', which represents the couple relationship. This is illustrated in the couple interview of Henry and Anne:

HENRY: I like, really like our cuddles or something where we just go to the bed and lie on the bed together and hug and –

ANNE: Yeah, kisses.

HENRY: Not particularly sexual, but just being very, very close, and, kind of, feeling, you know, um, feeling our bodies next to each [other] I think it's very bodily, but it's not necessarily sexual, it's just about being close and very comfortable with each other.

ANNE: Yeah, I might touch your tummy [laughing] or something like that. **HENRY**: Yeah, it's nice.

For Henry, the shift from the singular to plural first-person pronoun works to consolidate the harmony of like minds, and like bodies. The fondness that is present in the exchange between Henry and Anne is unmistakeable, with both parties crafting a shared couple story that is knitted together through their mutual interjections. Their dialogue also reinforces the often keenly felt distinction between physical intimacy and sex. Embodied affection is characterised as crucial to Henry and Anne's relationship whereas the vagaries of their sex life is of a secondary order, a distinction that was even more categorically stated by another couple, Rose and Hugh:

ROSE: [Sex] is one of the prerequisites of a relationship for me, and I think for you. But there are other areas of a relationship which I think are … need a lot more work, and are far more important … like trust, money, love, teamwork.

HUGH: There are things that are more enduring.

Sentiments such as these were echoed by many participants. Sex was identified as one factor among many others in the couple relationship mix. There were other qualities and relationship practices which were 'enduring' and which enabled a relationship to endure. This does not, however, diminish the significance of sex, but instead situates it *in context*, that is to say in the broader context of the couple relationship narrative. In the following section we focus on the in/significance of sex in order to unpick its meanings in long-term couple relationships. In so doing, we draw attention to the factors which impact on couple's sex lives and how couples work together to negotiate such eventualities.

The in/significance of sex

Survey responses to the question 'Sex is an important part of your relationship?' tell an incontrovertible story about sex and the couple relationship, graphically demonstrated in Figure 4.1.

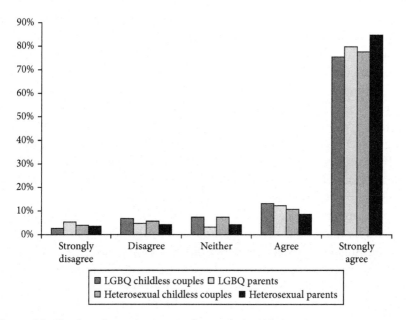

Figure 4.1 Sex is an important part of our relationship

The National Survey of Sexual Attitudes and Lifestyles (Natsal) has provided detailed data on sexual behaviour in contemporary Britain. Three waves of Natsal surveys have taken place: Natsal-1 in 1990–1991, Natsal-2 in 1999–2001 and Natsal-3 in 2010–2012. From these longitudinal datasets it is claimed that women's sexual behaviour has changed over the past ten years, with an increase in the number of sexual partners and sexual experimentation. The gender-neutral responses to the *Enduring Love?* survey question on the significance of sex thus appear to support the attitudinal shift reported by Natsal. When we examine the responses to other related questions, however, this consensus and allied 'progressive' attitude begin to unravel. Indeed, responses to the statement 'My partner wants to have sex more often than I do' reveal a far more traditional picture, with answers being clearly differentiated by gender and parenthood. Women (mothers and childfree) were most likely to agree with this statement. Men (fathers and childfree) were most likely to disagree with it. When gender and parenthood were combined, differences became even more significant.[2] Mothers were four times more likely than fathers to agree with this assertion. The number of children living within the family also seemed to have a larger and significantly more adverse effect on mothers than on fathers. Relationship duration likewise appeared to have an impact, with greater relationship longevity corresponding with a decrease in congruence around sexual desire. There were several additional factors which differentiated responses still further, namely residency and sexual orientation.[3] Those who were 'going out' or did not live with their partner (living apart together (LAT) couples) were the most likely to indicate congruence in sexual frequency and desire in their relationships; likewise, LGBQ couples – both parents and childfree. It was couples in married heterosexual relationships who were the most likely to perceive the most significant differences in sexual frequency and desire.

There are several explanations that might account for such findings. It could be that sexual scripts (Simon & Gagnon, 2003) in heterosexual relationships both reflect gendered differences and serve to cleave apart lives and experience already crafted as distinct – corroborating the cultural rhetoric of 'men are from Mars, women are from Venus'. Alternatively, women, as wives and mothers, may be adhering to a socio-cultural script wherein bemoaning the shortcomings of men is expected. In some ways we can only speculate explanations for these particular survey findings.

Other survey data do, however, point to the resilience of stereotypical gendered attitudes. For example, in response to the question 'What does your partner do for you that makes you feel appreciated?',[4] men (child-free and fathers) were three times more likely than women (childfree and mothers) to mention sexual intimacy. A considerable degree of caution is arguably required before advancing straightforward gendered readings of such data. Critical analysis of sex research has shown that men are more inclined to overstate their sexual activity in sex surveys whereas women tend to downplay this dimension of their relationship (Stephenson & Sullivan, 2009). Survey findings, therefore, tell us just as much about the cultural constitution of sex and prevailing patriarchal norms as they do about sexual attitudes and practice.

Our analysis of the *Enduring Love?* survey data on sexual desire and frequency is, therefore, situated in this socio-cultural context. Moreover, and of crucial importance, while previous research has shown a correlation between relationship and sexual frequency satisfaction (Smith et al., 2011) this was not borne out in our data. For both mothers and fathers, dissatisfaction with sexual frequency did not appear to undermine overall (high levels of) relationship and partner satisfaction. It would appear that for mothers and fathers who took part in our survey, fluctuations in desire and sexual activity were understood as a component part of the parenting couple partnership and as such did not, per se, lead to relationship dissatisfaction.

Responses to the survey questions serve to instantiate a picture of sex and couple intimacy that is articulated through gender but which cannot be reduced to this. For example, for women, heterosexual and LGBQ alike, when describing what makes them feel appreciated, sexual intimacy was typically characterised in loving terms with the emotional meanings of sex being often emphasised.

He makes an effort and wants to please me when we make love
We have wonderful sex very often – it makes me feel loved and cared for
He's interested in me sexually after years together

In these women's responses, their partner's attentiveness to their needs was perceived as highly significant, with selflessness and generosity being repeatedly singled out. Another recurrent feature, as the responses above illustrate, was a sense of gratitude for continuing sexual attraction, over time, 'after years together'. Such a focus on appearance demonstrates pervasive – and invidious – socio-cultural norms which associate women's physical beauty with youthfulness, while men's attractiveness draws on their social status and power beyond embodied years. Thus it is unsurprising that there were no corresponding comments from men on ageing and their physical appearance. Heterosexual men's comments in this vein tended to focus on their partner's continuing desire to look attractive (for them) and/or her compliance with their sexual desire and preferences. Here, responding to the question 'What does your partner do for you that makes you feel appreciated?', the focus was on the sex act and included sometimes blunt – or even brutal – descriptions that lacked any relational dimension.

> Oral sex
> Is almost always prepared to have sex
> Has sex when she doesn't really want to

In these survey responses of heterosexual men, sex appeared to be used as a dispassionate commodity. Such answers seem diametrically opposed to the egalitarian ideals and 'pure relationship' era (Giddens, 1992) that are professed to characterise contemporary relationships in western culture. They are more akin to data found in earlier studies of 'his and her marriages' (Duncombe & Marsden, 1996; Mansfield & Collard, 1988). Sex is presented in selfish terms, couched in the discourses of individual need with no regard for the other's feelings. It is also pertinent to note here that different forms of sexual practice were afforded different value. Engaging in 'oral sex' was seen as a favour rather than part of everyday sexual practice, something which the partner does *for you* rather than *with you*. The anonymity afforded by the online survey may have facilitated such candour; there was, after all, no researcher present and no traceable connection back to the words spoken. As such there was perhaps less ownership of the statements registered.

There were, however, some responses by men that were compassionate and far more fondly phrased. For example:

> Hot sex and cups of tea ... great combination

While it may focus on the act of 'hot sex', this response shows no sign of disparagement and the sentiments are anything but dispassionate. The pleasures of a cup of tea featured with regularity and remained a highly meaningful and often jealously guarded dimension of the couple relationship, as discussed in other chapters. Here, for this male participant, the combination of sex and the totemic cup of tea appears to epitomise relationship satisfaction. An older heterosexual male participant who was in a relationship of over 20 years, he seems to celebrate and cherish the *extra*ordinariness of this combination and his response is steeped in wit and affection. It is important, therefore, not to polarise gendered responses. Marked differences did characterise some answers, but this does not tell the whole relationship story. Yet there is another factor that *did* seem to set apart one group of answers: parenthood. The responses of both mothers *and* fathers brought into stark relief the impact of having children on the sex lives of the parenting couple.

Sex and parenting

The greediness of parenthood in terms of time and energy, and the 'cost' of this on the couple partnership provides the experiential backdrop and context for the study's survey data. The statistical significance of the intersections of gender and parenthood was incontrovertible (Gabb et al., 2013), with free-text responses to the open questions highlighting the adverse impact that children have on the couple relationship dynamic and experiences of sexual intimacy.

> We don't have sex very often (small children) and we don't talk about this
> Our sex life is not great since having children

How couples work to manage the tensions between parenthood and partnership was addressed in the qualitative dimension of the study. Here, findings corroborate the wealth of research that points to the pressures that young children bring to bear on the couple relationship (Marshall, 2013; Walker et al., 2010) and the intimate couple (Gabb, 2008).) In practical terms, the impacts of sharing the 'marital' bed with children – when they are sick, upset or want a cuddle and company – were undoubtedly testing for many of the parenting couples. For some, this was perceived in stark terms, with children being seen as a wedge that served to physically and emotionally prise apart the couple.

Feminist research has drawn attention to the intersections of gender and power in shaping heterosexual relationships (Jackson, 1999; Meadows, 1997), while a focus on gendered inequalities in household relationships has shown how women's double bind as wives and mothers shapes their personal relationships, both inside and outside the home (Hochschild, 1989, 2003). Such gendered patterns in couple relationship experience were typically present in the interview data, being manifest in many different forms. In the context of relationship practices more particularly, the picture was often messy and emotionally complicated.

LOUISE: I think Luke would like to have sex more, it's not that I would like to have sex less, but I am less bothered ... I'm not frustrated I suppose with my lack of it.

LUKE: You also engineer it so we can't. So to be fair [...] You will only have sex if you have a bath, are in bed by ten, you know, all of these conditions which will never happen. So basically, you said, you know, every blue [moon] I'll have sex with you ...

LOUISE: That's the rule.

LUKE: Except of course it never happens.

For parents of young children like Louise and Luke, the intersections of power and sex were often writ large and couples were painfully aware of the detrimental impact this had on their formerly equal partnership. Though the exchange above is shrouded in banter and good-humoured repartee, tensions nevertheless remain. For Louise and Luke, sex has become a vehicle through which other underlying resentments are acted out, taking on a particularly powerful and symbolic function. Both partners talked about being simply exhausted from juggling work, family life and practical childcare responsibilities. When opportunities arose or when 'couple time' was carved out, however, Louise simply felt unable or perhaps unwilling to switch between multiple and different personae:

LOUISE: I don't have, almost have that energy to kind of shift from just being the knackered person who's just been at work all day and then tried to put the kids to bed, into kind of wife and lover [...] I have to make a mental transfer [...] If I'm knackered, and I'm not saying this is good, it's not a good thing, but sometimes I can't be arsed [...]

LUKE: But you know [...] I think it's partly a power thing.

LOUISE: Yeah, I'm sure there's an element of that.

In the course of their interviews the couple proceeded to talk about how sex was being used as an emotional and practical means to redress Louise's sense of 'powerlessness' at work, in her career and in her role at home, as primary childcare provider. There was a tangible sense of underlying distress and resentment in Louise's comments about the sacrifice of a fast-track career with all the self-esteem this bestows; the drudgeries of daily childcare responsibilities that characterise and overwhelm her; an imagined future of success and professional kudos side-lined before it even started. Sex thus affords Louise a means to take control. Her sexual resistance wrests power away from her partner and affords her some sense of embodied agency and power over her otherwise fraught and frustrated life. In Luke's individual data, however, he raised the impact that Louise's strategic behaviour was having on him. Working excessively long hours to establish a professional career, tensions within this couple relationship were starkly presented. Both parties were struggling equally in their own ways to keep the different and often competing dimensions of their work–family–personal lives in balance. Equilibrium was rare. However, what appears to enable this couple to 'hang in there' is their shared underlying belief that their present-day lives and lifestyles are temporary. This moment in time does not epitomise their long-term relationship. As a couple they currently lack resources, due to having young children and both working in time-greedy careers, but they both want to, and can, see beyond this point in time. Their couple relationship is more, and worth more, than this.

For Louise and Luke, the importance of the relationship horizon was crucial in their reflections on relationship longevity. Their relationship was sometimes characterised as years to come, in other instances

it was just around the corner, in the here and now, conjured from sto-
len moments that transported the couple out of the everyday humdrum
of their otherwise busy lives. In such instances, sexual desire happily
returned, once tiredness subsided and the ebbs and flows of couple time
was re-established.

LOUISE: Feels like a real holiday not having [children] here (though I
           do miss them). [Partner] and I have lazy hour in bed in the
           morning which we never usually get and have sex for the first
           time in a week or so. We go out for a lovely breakfast with the
           Saturday paper at a local greasy spoon café and get on really
           well.

These data illustrate the significance of temporality in understanding
couple relationships. When the knotted threads of parenting and partner-
ing can be teased apart, precious time affords opportunities to rediscover
intimacy, sex and simply being together. For this couple, parenthood
poses a range of practical challenges, not least to sexual intimacy, but
it does not define their couple relationship. Imagining the relationship
horizon enables them to keep going, to invest in their lives together – for
the long haul. There is a sense in the data, then, that parenting couples
develop resilience through holding onto the longed-for and imagined
relationship horizon, keeping it secure through the immediacy of small
moments of intimacy in the here and now. The intersections of time and
space are crucial in couples' management of this imagined project, serving to ground what might otherwise be ephemeral and precarious.

Making space for intimacy

As we discussed in Chapter 2, feeling 'at home' with yourself and the
couple relationship was often situated at the core of what couples in the
Enduring Love? study valued about their life together. Home was crucial in both holding and containing experiences of couple intimacy and
sexual relations that were, in turn, routinely shaped by the physical envi-
ronments in which couples lived and loved at different points in the life

course. Home functions as a sign that is loaded with connotation (Gabb, 2008) wherein understandings of home equate with a series of overlapping front and back stages (Morgan, 1996) which are structured along a public–private axis (Allan & Crow, 1989). In families, ideas of propriety inform the use of rooms and shore up distinctions between parents and children by constructing boundaries around sex and intimacy (Gabb, 2013). Separate spaces that may appear mutually exclusive if charted on a two-dimensional map are simultaneously occupied on an everyday level (Rose, 1993, pp. 140–159). Data from the study revealed that couple space and/or a space associated with sexual intimacy were often squeezed to the very limits of sustainability in family households, as Debs clearly demonstrated when talking through her emotion map data (Figure 4.2).

DEBS: The kitchen is the heart of the home – it clearly is! [Laughs] …
          I don't think any of the spaces feel hugely private or coupley.
          Our bedroom certainly doesn't because the kids play in the
          bed the whole time; it's one of their favourite places to play.

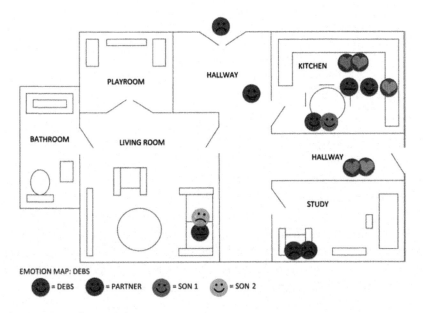

Figure 4.2   Debs' emotion map

The kitchen, and relationship practices such as eating together at the kitchen or dining room table, featured in many accounts of couple experience and/or imaginings of what intimate life could or should be in the future, if circumstances allowed. Moments of couple intimacy featured in Debs' emotion map are located in the kitchen as the couple shared a snatched embrace, and in the hallway as they swapped over household 'shifts', leaving for and returning from work. For Debs and her partner, these moments of reunion at the beginning and end of the day were described with great fondness. The children's excitement at seeing the returning parent was highly cherished. As we noted in Chapter 1, ideas of home across the study's dataset were perceived as crucial in sustaining the couple relationship. In the context of family households that included children, couple space was often impossible to keep private, but protecting couple intimacy appeared less important in these circumstances, as Debs illustrates, than building a sense of togetherness into the fabric of the home, where all parties could grow together and be together.

> Debs: Yes, hugely important, yeah. No I think home is – you know, we're both quite homey. It's far more than a place to lay your head, yeah. And we love this house … we moved here and within two weeks I was pregnant which you know, felt very psychologically – very significant in terms of you know I felt so 'at home' that I was able to get pregnant [laughs]. And then I lost that baby, so it's not quite such a nice story, but you know it's kind of part of our story about how right this place feels to us and how important it is to us to live here. Not just in the house but in the wider community and the wider sense. We feel very settled – we both feel very settled, yeah, and that's important.

Debs' couple biography is built into the bricks and mortar of the home she and her partner share. For another recently married couple, this idea of home featured centrally in the ways they imagined their long-term relationship. At the point of interview, the couple had just made the decision to buy a house together and they were actively looking for a property that would accommodate their needs as a newly-wed couple. In her descriptions of this imagined place, Anna does not fantasise a cereal box ideal of coupledom, but a place that *fits* the relationship needs and desires of her and her partner. Whereas Debs portrays a home in which couple intimacy wraps around the exigencies of parenting, the home that Anna imagines provides a privacy and permanency that she longs for, an environment that will comfortably accommodate the couple's future family lives alongside their open sexually permissive relationship.

ANNA: I want to live in my house for about 30, 40 years. I don't want to sell and move again! Which means I have to think, well, actually if we're ever going to have children, we're going have to have at least a three-bedroomed house, because it gives us the space to grow [...] Our house is going to be [...] somewhere that reflects us, that we can use as we need to, or as we want to [...] our sexual activities are very restricted by this house, incredibly restricted, because we can't put any solid ... anchor points in [...] you put an anchor point in a floor (here) and someone else comes in and goes, 'What's that there? Why is that there?' [...] It's that opportunity to be able to say, okay, let's tailor the house to us, and to what we want to do with it and how we want to conduct our lives in it, so that it becomes our space and not just [...] the place we happen to live in.

The home being described here by Anna is, therefore, performing vital relationship work, in that it both allows the couple to live the relationship that they both want, individually and together, and accommodates their future plans which include parenthood. While parents in the study acknowledged the impossibility of parent–partner distinctions in the uses of the home's spatial dimensions, childfree younger couples were inclined to imagine a compartmentalised future for the different elements of their everyday life. Anna's soon-to-be purchased home thus allowed the possibility of disentangling the couple's material, planned and fantasy lives together. Here, the public–private axis (Allan & Crow, 1989) is not refuted or ignored; instead it is fashioned into a multidimensional helix that enabled Anna to reconcile and embrace the different emotional/practical, maternal/sexual and adult/child areas of her life. Parenthood, partners, children, sex and sexuality are mutually situated within Anna's spatio-temporal 'frame': a shifting scaffold that in many ways resists simple categorisation. The arrival of a child is highly likely to muddy her clearly defined imagined boundaries, but what her account demonstrates is how home is invoked to positively hold the couple relationship and personal experiences of intimacy therein.

In other circumstances, where resources and cultural capital were less freely available, the inadequacies of space, the precariousness of tenancy agreements and the inability to call a space their own adversely impacted on how couples could inhabit their households and experience intimate life together.

INTERVIEWER: So what would help you feel more secure?
KRIS: Being employed for one. I think, if you spend too much time in the same house with each other, you get under each other's feet. And that's just, that causes arguments. I know that … that happens with a lot of couples, that you do need time away, not large amounts of time but time to do your own things as well as do things together …

[My dream home] would be nothing flash or extravagant, just something with a bit of space, so that, you know, if [child] wants to go to her room somewhere, she can go to there without [other child] following her. Or space to put things or, you know, a bit of a garden or something so they can have a bit of fun in the summer.

For couples like Kris and his partner, critical intersections of time and space highlight how resources converge to shape the couple relationship both in terms of what is experienced and what can be imagined. While Anna conjures a future where time and space, home and intimacy can be fashioned and secured, Kris struggles to grasp security for himself and his family. Endless time together does not engender quality couple time; instead, it leads to arguments. Restrictions of space and the pressures of having to share a bedroom with young children inevitably take a heavy toll on couple relationships. Household space and relationship practices which some couples take for granted are simply unavailable or even unimaginable for others. Welfare reforms which imposed a 'bedroom tax' (2013) have served to make hard lives even harder. For socially disadvantaged couples, retaining any sense of discrete couple time and/or privacy of space for intimacy can feel impossible.

As the above examples illustrate, home represents far more than a place to lay your head and/or for a couple to live together; it is experienced as part of who the couple is, and, in the context of this chapter, how each partner experiences physical affection and sexual intimacy. There may be multiple configurations of intimacy and physical affection and great variations in sexual practice, but to sustain a couple relationship these dimensions require space to accommodate them. Space also enables couples to adapt, emotionally and physically, to the changes that occur across the life course and the resulting effects that these have on their relationship.

Ageing bodies and relationship duration

Facing the challenges and opportunities posed by long-term relationships was something that at times vexed couples as they sought to manage the sexual problems that accompany ageing and the disruptions these heralded for established patterns of intimacy.

TED: Since [I've been unwell], I have to admit to being impotent, so – so admitting to impotency, I, we did sleep in the same bed for some time but then agreed I went into the smaller bedroom because we were more comfortable. We could roll about at our own will and so on. I could get up if I wanted to. [Partner] could get up and do whatever. And we're perfectly happy with that. We weren't happy that we couldn't share, you know, our physical relationship in that way, but every night we do say we love each other.

In this interview extract, Ted's description of his impotency and its effects highlights a crucial change which is so often an unspoken dimension of couple relationships and which, therefore, has to be 'admitted'. Being impotent disrupts not only socio-cultural norms of coupledom, in which a sexual relationship is central, but also related ideas and meanings around the conjugal bed as a space in which a couple's respective sexual needs are met. This is reflected in Ted's concern to provide reasons for no longer sleeping in the same bed as his partner, which largely elide the absence of any sexual intimacy in their lives and focus instead on the way *separate* bedrooms allow them to be more comfortable and avoid disruptions to each other's sleep patterns. By vacating their shared bed and thus distancing himself from regular close physical contact with his partner, Ted may arguably feel more able to manage the emotional difficulties he experiences around his impotency and its impact on his relationship. These sleeping arrangements, while not a panacea for this change in their life together, have allowed Ted to fashion other practices through which he can demonstrate his continuing love and affection for his wife, one of which, as he touchingly states, is the night-time routine of declaring their love for each other.

When men's accounts of ageing included the lessening of sexual inclination and/or health issues such as impotency, sentiments remained raw and were often framed by the male participant as a personal failing. Trying to stave off the cultural spectre that associates masculinity with sex drive, between the lines and in their text these men typically presented deeply vulnerable personae. Notwithstanding a supportive and understanding partner, there was a tangible sense of men feeling disappointed in themselves and their perceived failure to meet what they understood to be the expectations of their partner and society. In other instances, however, accommodating changes brought on by an ageing body that fails to keep pace with both emotional and physical desires, the relationship appeared to be enriched as the couple embarked on joint endeavours to find solutions that worked for both parties. Here, intimate knowledge and trust were crucial factors in couples' 'coping' strategies, so too humour.

CLIVE: We don't feel the need to have sex all the time because I think after 13 years, you know [...] it's just an extension of the way we are with each other [...] but even then sometimes, you know, the fact of the way you are it's not a pressure, even then you can find a comedy element sort of creep in because you can find you're trying to be intimate but you're having a battle with the bedclothes, which is kind of like there's three of us in this relationship – me, you and the duvet – and it's like we might as well give up.

> And you can have that laugh because there isn't the pres-
> sure of like, 'We must have it now.'

For this gay couple, being able to laugh about changes in their sex life makes the situation both safe and enjoyable. Their intimate knowledge of each other enables them to enjoy the playfulness of the moment, sexual or otherwise. Responding to the sex and intimacy collage which included the front covers of various relationship handbooks, another couple likewise drew in humour and light-hearted banter to regale their sexual story.

MARGARET: *The Sex Starved Marriage.* Oh you can relate to that, poor [partner], after my hormones packed up [...] We used to have baths together but we don't bother with that any-more. It takes so much time [...] We have showers instead of baths. The older you get the less time we have for things [...]

MARTIN: We had one or two books that we were looking at.

MARGARET: But sex is so painful now that it isn't adventurous anymore.

MARTIN: You tend to sort of do it for my benefit rather than for yourself, don't you? But you seem to enjoy it. You're good at conning me if you're not.

MARGARET: Well I make the best of it shall I say [...] I think compan-ionship creates a lot of intimacy [...] I think we've got a lot of intimacy [...]

MARTIN: I was quite surprised at myself that I haven't lost my desire if you like, without using medicine [...]

MARGARET: It is once every week or once a fortnight. So you might be likely more, not sex starved, but slightly sex hungry at times.

For Margaret and Martin, their mismatch in sexual desire is managed through affectionate banter but this is not used to make light of a difficult issue; instead, their shared humour and sense of fun render it a safe topic for discussion.

MARGARET: Martin makes it fun because we have a joke as well, don't
              we. We laugh. So instead of being passionate it is quite
              entertaining. [Laughter]
MARTIN: Yes.
MARGARET: It's not boring.
MARTIN: I try to make a variation and jokes and stuff.

The relationship work that both parties are doing here, both in the interview and in their sex lives, is palpable. Their laughter is not derisory but
a consequence of mutual fondness. The first blush of a new relationship may have worn off but the relationship has not tarnished. Newness
has been replaced by treasured familiarity: their pleasure in a shared life
together. While the sex issue may have otherwise put great stress on the
couple relationship, overcoming the problem has served to strengthen
their partnership and evident commitment to each other and the couple
project.

Older couples often spoke about drawing on the shared resources and
'wisdom' accrued through past experiences. This time in life was just one
chapter in a much longer relationship narrative. For 'second time rounders' such temporal continuities were absent, but past experiences were
not necessarily cast aside. Starting afresh was perceived as an opportunity to reflect on and cherish time that might hitherto have passed by
unnoticed. While the general trend in divorce rates is downward, towards
the upper age ranges there is an increase (ONS, 2012). For some, this
so-called grey divorce was not associated with endings or an unhappy
finishing point. This point in their life course signalled a chance for new
beginnings: a time to start investing in a new relationship and building
a future together, second time round. For example, Hayley, a 'second
time rounder', painted a picture that was rich in literal and metaphorical
'fresh shoots'. Their garden and growing menagerie had provided a site
of nurturing for their relationship. This embodied investment in a joint
endeavour held the potential to flourish, over time, through their physical and emotional attention.

HAYLEY: I went downstairs and made breakfast for us which we ate
              in the garden. Since moving in last Oct. we have worked

hard on making the garden nice. We tour the garden together every day to see how things are: veggies growing, chickens happy, plants taken etc. We do this whilst talking about our plans for the future.

Second time rounders like Hayley were not lamenting past failed relationships or rushing to catch up on missed opportunities; instead, there was a sense that these couples enjoyed taking time, pausing for reflection and appreciating what they had in life rather than taking things for granted. In this context, perhaps, couples brought to the relationship knowledge gained from previous relationships: lessons learned. There was, in many ways then, a greater appreciation of time spent together in these couples. Associations of mid- and later-life with a dwindling interest in sex did characterise many couples in this age cohort but other data served to counter cultural myths about ageing and decreased sexual desire. As children left home or the pressures of career and home life became more equally balanced, relationships could take on a 'second life'.

NINA: I think it's got better and better. I think it's deeper, in a funny sort of way. I think as we've matured […] I can't help thinking it's about coupling and uncoupling. So the more, in a way, autonomous an individual you are, the more the coming together can be rich and deep, and actually, I think it keeps us going [… Sex] hasn't always been as frequent as it is now, which is interesting, isn't it? When we were younger it was a lot less frequent, because we were both working hard full-time and were knackered, basically.

Rather than familiarity and its association with boredom adversely affecting couple intimacy, Nina suggests that deep knowing and sharing a life (and love) together can *enrich* the sexual relationship. Over the passage of time and with the increased availability of couple time, the intimate connection between Nina and her partner has been enhanced and strengthened. Whether a new relationship second time round, or the second life that can accompany the post-parenthood era, the opportunities offered by these *second chances* were typically warmly embraced and welcomed. Couples appeared to relish finding ways to accommodate changes in personality, interests, physical abilities and circumstances within the dynamic couple relationship. Sexual intimacy was embedded into the broader fabric of what worked for each couple and their particular relationship narrative.

MOLLY: I think as, as it gets further along you get, you've had more shared experiences so you've got more things to kind of pull upon […] when you're first together and it's all exciting and new […] that's just a change, that it's not necessarily a bad thing. You're not kind of panicking that like, 'Oh well, you know, we used to have sex all the time and now we don't because –'. But, just seeing that things, things change as the relationship kind of matures and sort of not seeing that as a negative, that's just kind of, that's how it changes because it's got to change.

The sentiments expressed here by Molly in many ways typify those articulated across the dataset. Sexual intimacy was one factor in the couple relationship. Fluctuations in desire were inexorably tied into other life factors, but it was the sharing of a life together, the investment in that joint venture and the acceptance that change is an integral part of this shared life which enabled couples to weather the ebbs and flows that characterise sexual intimacy and the passage of time in long-term relationships.

Notes

1. See Appendix 2, Table A2.1: 'What does your partner do for you that makes you feel appreciated?'
2. See Appendix 2, Table A2.5: 'My partner wants to have sex more often than I do' by gender and parenthood.
3. See Appendix 2, Table A2.6: 'My partner wants to have sex more often than I do' by relationship status and residency; and Table A2.7: 'My partner wants to have sex more often than I do' by parenthood and sexuality.

4. See Appendix 2, Table A2.1: 'What does your partner do for you that makes you feel appreciated?'

References

Allan, G., & Crow, G. (1989). Insiders and Outsiders: Boundaries Around the Home. In G. Allan & G. Crow (Eds.), *Home and Family*. Basingstoke: Macmillan.

Barker, M., & Langdridge, D. (2008). Bisexuality: Working with a Silenced Sexuality. *Feminism & Psychology, 18*(3), 389–394.

Berlant, L. (1997). *The Queen of America Goes to Washington City. Essays on Sex and Citizenship*. Durham, NC: Duke University Press.

Berlant, L., & Edelman, L. (2013). *Sex, or the Unbearable*. Durham, NC: Duke University Press.

Duncombe, J., & Marsden, D. (1996). 'Whose Orgasm Is This Anyway?' 'Sex Work' in Long-Term Heterosexual Couple Relationships. In J. Weeks & J. Holland (Eds.), *Sexual Cultures: Communities, Values and Intimacy* (pp. 220–238). Basingstoke: Macmillan.

Frank, A., Clough, P. T., & Seidman, S. (Eds.). (2013). *Intimacies. A New World of Relational Life*. New York: Routledge.

Frye, M. (1991). Lesbian 'Sex'. In J. Barrington (Ed.), *An Intimate Wilderness. Lesbian Writers on Sexuality* (pp. 1–8). Portland, OR: The Eighth Mountain Press.

Gabb, J. (2008). *Researching Intimacy in Families*. Basingstoke: Palgrave Macmillan.

Gabb, J. (2011). Family Lives and Relational Living: Taking Account of Otherness. *Sociological Research Online, 16*(4). Retrieved from http://www.socresonline.org.uk/16/14/10.html

Gabb, J. (2013). Embodying Risk: Managing Father–Child Intimacy and the Display of Nudity in Families. *Sociology, 47*(4), 639–654.

Gabb, J., Klett-Davies, M., Fink, J., & Thomae, M. (2013). *Enduring Love? Couple Relationships in the 21st Century. Survey Findings Report*. Milton Keynes: The Open University. Retrieved from http://www.open.ac.uk/researchprojects/enduringlove/files/enduringlove/file/ecms/web-content/Final-Enduring-Love-Survey-Report.pdf

Giddens, A. (1992). *The Transformation of Intimacy: Sexuality, Love and Eroticism in Modern Societies*. Cambridge: Polity Press.

Gillis, J. R. (1996). *A World of Their Own Making. A History of Myth and Ritual in Family Life.* Oxford: Oxford University Press.

Grosz, E. (1993). Merleau-Ponty and Irigaray in the Flesh. *Thesis Eleven, 36,* 37–59.

Heaphy, B., & Einarsdottir, A. (2013). Scripting Civil Partnerships: Interviewing Couples Together and Apart. *Qualitative Research, 13*(1), 53–70.

Heaphy, B., Smart, C., & Einarsdottir, A. (2013). *Same Sex Marriages: New Generations, New Relationships.* Basingstoke: Palgrave Macmillan.

Hesse-Biber, S. (2010). Emerging Methodologies and Methods in the Field of Mixed Methods Research. *Qualitative Inquiry, 16*(6), 415–418.

Hochschild, A. R. (1989). *The Second Shift: Working Parents and the Revolution at Home.* New York, NY: Viking.

Hochschild, A. R. (2003). *The Commercialization of Intimate Life: Notes from Home and Work.* Berkeley: University of California Press.

Hockey, J., Meah, A., & Robinson, V. (2010). *Mundane Heterosexualities: From Theory to Practices.* Basingstoke: Palgrave Macmillan.

Jackson, S. (1999). *Heterosexuality in Question.* London: Sage.

Johnson, P. (2005). *Love, Heterosexuality and Society: Sociological Perspectives on Love and Heterosexuality.* Basingstoke: Palgrave Macmillan.

Kimmel, M. (Ed.). (2007). *The Sexual Self. The Construction of Sexual Scripts.* Nashville, TN: Vanderbilt University Press.

Kinsey, A., Pomeroy, W. B., & Martin, C. E. (1948). *Sexual Behaviour in the Human Male.* Philadelphia: W. B. Saunders.

Kinsey, A., Pomeroy, W. B., Martin, C. E., & Gebhard, P. H. (1953). *Sexual Behaviour in the Human Female.* Philadelphia: W. B. Saunders.

Koedt, A. (1973). The Myth of the Vaginal Orgasm. In A. Koedt, E. Levine, & A. Rapone (Eds.), *Radical Feminism* (pp. 198–207). New York: Quadrangle Books.

Langford, W. (1999). *Revolutions of the Heart. Gender, Power and the Delusions of Love.* London: Routledge.

Mansfield, P., & Collard, J. (1988). *The Beginning of the Rest of Your Life?* London: Macmillan.

Marshall, A. G. (2013). *I Love You But You Always Put Me Last: How to Childproof Your Marriage.* London: Macmillan.

Masters, W. H., & Johnson, V. E. (1966). *Human Sexual Response.* Boston: Little Brown and Co.

Masters, W. H., & Johnson, V. E. (1970). *Human Sexual Inadequacy.* Boston: Little Brown and Co.

Meadows, M. (1997). Exploring the Invisible: Listening to Mid-Life Women about Heterosexual Sex. *Women's Studies International Forum, 20*(1), 145–152.

Morgan, D. H. J. (1996). *Family Connections: An Introduction to Family Studies.* Cambridge: Polity Press.

NATSAL. (2013). *The Third National Survey of Sexual Attitudes and Lifestyles.* The Lancet. Retrieved from http://www.thelancet.com/themed/natsal.

ONS. (2012). *Divorces in England and Wales – 2011. Statistical Bulletin.* Retrieved from http://www.ons.gov.uk/ons/dcp171778_291750.pdf

Plummer, K. (1995). *Telling Sexual Stories: Power, Change and Social Worlds.* London: Routledge.

Rahman, M., & Jackson, S. (2010). *Sexuality and Gender. Sociological Perspectives.* London: Polity.

Rich, A. (1980). Compulsory Heterosexuality and Lesbian Existence. *Signs, 5*(4), 631–660.

Rose, G. (1993). *Feminism and the Limits of Geographical Knowledge.* Cambridge: Polity Press.

Simon, W., & Gagnon, J. (2003). Sexual Scripts: Origins, Influences and Changes. *Qualitative Sociology, 26*(4), 491–497.

Smart, C. (2007). *Personal Life.* Cambridge: Polity Press.

Smith, A., Lyons, A., Ferris, J., Richters, J., Pitts, M., Shelley, J., & Simpson, J. M. (2011). Sexual and Relationship Satisfaction Among Heterosexual Men and Women: The Importance of Desired Frequency of Sex. *Journal of Sex & Marital Therapy, 37*(2), 104–115.

Stein, A. (1997). *Sex and Sensibility: Stories of a Lesbian Generation.* Berkeley: University of California Press.

Stephenson, K. R., & Sullivan, K. T. (2009). Social Norms and General Sexual Satisfaction: The Cost of Misperceived Descriptive Norms. *The Canadian Journal of Human Sexuality, 18*(3), 89–105.

Walker, J., Barrett, H., Wilson, G., & Chang, Y.-S. (2010). *Understanding the Needs of Adults (Particularly Parents) Regarding Relationship Support. Research Brief DCSF-RBX-10-01.* London: DCFS.

Wilton, T. (1996). Which One's the Man? The Heterosexualisation of Lesbian Sex. In D. Richardson (Ed.), *Theorising Heterosexuality* (pp. 125–142). Milton Keynes: Open University Press.

5

Unsettling Coupledom

There has been an intimate turn in sociological analyses of relationships (Gabb, 2008), suggesting that who and how we love is founded on the principles of mutuality and reciprocity, reflecting a 'wholesale democratisation of the interpersonal domain' (Giddens, 1992, p. 3). While the orthodoxy of such change has been effectively contested (Jamieson, 1999), there is general agreement that there has been a paradigm shift in the traditional patterning of intimacy. People's intimate networks resist unitary relational categories (Williams, 2004), comprising family-like (Weeks, Heaphy, & Donovan, 2001) and beyond family (Jamieson et al., 2006; Roseneil & Budgeon, 2004) affinities. Relationships are multifaceted and draw on symbolic, crafted, emotional and embodied affinities (Mason, 2008) that are concretised and attributed meaning in different ways and in different individual/social contexts, affectively shaping familial inter-subjectivity through a sense of relationality (Smart, 2007). This conceptual shift onto processes and practices (Morgan, 1996) has not been replicated in studies of couple relationships. As we noted in Chapter 1, couple relationships are all too often carved up into different types of couple, whether this is through parenthood, sexual orientation, generation, open versus monogamous relationships and so on.

© The Author(s) 2018
J. Gabb, J. Fink, *Couple Relationships in the 21st Century*, Palgrave Macmillan Studies in Family and Intimate Life, DOI 10.1007/978-3-319-59698-3_5

Ideas of 'the couple' remain prevalent in the cultural imaginary, social policy and legislation, professional practice and relationship support and, perhaps most surprisingly, in academic analyses across the disciplinary spectrum. The queer critique of coupledom has sought to prise apart meanings and understandings of 'the couple', with recent developments in UK civil partnership and same-sex marriage legislation giving new vigour and increased impetus to this venture. Work in this vein has interrogated and challenged the discourses that serve to marginalise non-dyadic relationships (Barker & Langdridge, 2010), demonstrating how social and welfare policies are being deployed to promote particular mononormative forms of intimacy (Smith, 2007). The queer provocation is, then, that 'compulsory heterosexuality' (Rich, 1980) has been superseded by 'compulsory coupledom' (Wilkinson, 2013). Sexual orientation is no longer relevant as the defining character of the relational unit. Transformations of intimacy and care have eroded the heterosexual/homosexual dichotomy (Roseneil, 2000), out of which comes 'a certain logic of congruence' (Weeks, Donovan, & Heaphy, 1999, p. 85). The 'good gay' has moved into the centre of the 'charmed circle' (Rubin, 1984), carried forwards on a tidal surge of love and all things procreative. The distinction that remains is between couples and the uncoupled (Wilkinson, 2013), with the ideology of couple culture (Budgeon, 2008) pushing aside all other relational alternatives through prohibition and marginalisation.

In the *Enduring Love?* study, narratives of 'the couple' were inevitably writ large with often a profound sense that there was something special, a *deeper* knowing, that existed between partners.

Joss: It's definitely about that kind of getting a reflection of yourself back from someone else. It's kind of, you know, two mirrors opposite each other that keep reflecting off each other, so, you know, I like the image of myself that I see in [partner]'s response to me. And he likes the image of him that he sees in my … in me in response to him […] there's something … that it's definitely allied to kind of sexual attraction […] that's a really important part of it in my mind; it's that kind of … it's why talking to [partner] is not like talking to some of my good friends with whom I also share intellectual interests. You know, but I don't fancy them, so it's just … it's just a really interesting conversation. But it hasn't got that kind of energy behind it, that … that talking to [partner] does have.

Such ideas of 'the one' persisted, at some level, in some shape or form for most couples. For Joss, as with most, if not all participants, the couple relationship was perceived and experienced – often in some intangible way – as special. Our point here is thus twofold. Firstly, the recognition of the couple relationship as something special does not serve to set it apart. This relationship is typically embedded within wider networks of intimacy (Jamieson, 2011). Without the love, support, intimacy and friendship of these significant others, couple relationships appear to be experienced as qualitatively poorer and less able to weather the stressors and adversities, and enjoy the pleasures and accomplishments, which couples ordinarily encounter. Secondly, notwithstanding the specialness of one's partner and/or the couple dynamic, in practice – or, more precisely, as stated in *relationship practices* – there is scant semblance of western cultural norms of 'the couple' (Stacey, 2011). As with families, it is couples rather than 'the couple' that reflect the relational experience. Moreover, differences and diversity cannot be easily mapped onto particular relationship forms (such as open/monogamous), groups of participants (young/old; heterosexual/queer), political convictions or beliefs (non-normative/traditional). Bearing in mind that our sampling strategy was driven by sociological demographic criteria and not diversity per se,[1] to find such diversity across the sample *without looking for it* is both significant and telling. In this chapter, therefore, we explore some of the critical junctures around which relationship diversity emerges and how these instances undo normative ideas of 'the couple' and the chimera of coupledom.

Our analysis in this chapter has been informed by the sociological thinking of Georg Simmel and his writing on dyads and triads. Simmel suggests that: 'A dyad depends on each of its two elements alone – in its death though not in its life: for its life it needs both, but for its death, only one' (2012 (1908), p. 384). The dyad is thus dependent on reciprocity; it requires commitment to the whole by each individual for the dyad to effectively operate. In this sense, it is simultaneously internally robust (nurtured and sustained by the commitment of both parties) and always fragile (if one party stops working at it, the whole – the couple dyad – becomes unstable). Through the addition of a third party, novel processes and actions are opened up (Coser, 1977). Simmel (2012 (1908)) identifies three such processes: a third party can act as a mediator through which tensions and disagreements can be filtered and assuaged; they can exploit unease within the dyad to bolster their own status and sense of security and/or actively exploit tensions in the dyad to enhance their own status. In our analysis of couple relationships, different dimensions of these three processes can, at times, be traced. Although the processes identified by Simmel were not originally or directly associated with couple relationships their relevance in this context still opens up productive analytical insights. They have helped us to expand our ways of framing couple relationships and, in so doing, reflect the diverse and dynamic configurations that are experienced.

Parenting

An expansion of both the conceptual imagination and understandings of couple relationships is required to accommodate the arrival (and needs) of another party within the dyadic unit. For parents, the couple dynamic must shift as a child becomes rooted within the fabric of their relationship. Ulrich Beck and Elisabeth Beck-Gernsheim suggest that parents' novel response to the emotional uncertainty and burgeoning individualism of twenty-first-century life means that they are turning to their children for lifelong commitment and love:

> [The child] promises a tie which is more elemental, profound and durable than any other in society [...] the ultimate guarantee of permanence, providing an anchor for one's life. (Beck & Beck-Gersheim, 1995, p. 73)

Social theorising in this vein has suggested that in the context of contemporary self-help culture (Giddens, 1992) and the breakdown of community and extended kin networks (Bauman, 2003; Beck, 2000), couple relationships are shaping and being shaped by a culture of individualisation. While empirical studies have usefully and compellingly highlighted the importance of connections and embeddedness as the structuring principles behind lived lives (Smart, 2007), there is a sense that people no longer depend on the adult couple as a permanent relationship 'til death do us part'.

Our study's survey sought to directly address the arguments for and against the individualisation thesis through the question: 'Who is the most important person in your life?' Participants could choose one item from the drop-down list which included children, partner, father, sister, other family members, friend, mother, brother, self and other. There were some significant differences in responses, with those of mothers and fathers being significantly gendered.[2] Mothers were almost twice more likely than fathers to select their child/ren as the most important person in their life, while fathers were far more likely to value their partners. As expected, with an increase in the age of child/ren there was a corresponding decrease in parents' selection of this answer, but again, the downward trend was distinctly gendered, being far steeper for fathers than for mothers. Moreover, in the relationship measures produced from the survey (Gabb et al., 2013), mothers scored significantly lower than child-free women on relationship quality, relationship with partner, relationship maintenance and happiness with relationship/partner. Paradoxically mothers recorded being significantly happier with life than any other group.[3] Whether these survey responses were a consequence of mothers' feelings, a record of their experience or the result of cultural norms cannot be known. What we can infer from these data is that, in contrast to fathers, for mothers children can be the primary source of happiness rather than their partner.

Participants were also asked to explain the rationale for their answer to this question about the most important person in their life. Many participants lamented the requirement to choose one person above another. For some, this prioritisation was characterised as untenable: their relationships were intertwined; feelings are not readily divisible or quantifiable. The question presented these respondents with a conundrum which they felt ill-equipped to resolve. For others, their answers revealed a high degree of reflexivity and pragmatic reasoning. Notwithstanding

the character of the justification, these responses illustrate how relationships with children and partner are differentiated. Participants who
chose child/ren felt that the love for a child is forever and unconditional;
a child can give one's own life meaning. Essentialist parental discourses
were typically invoked, citing the importance of so-called blood ties and
a child being part of one's self.

> Because my son is the reason for being
>   I could never walk away. I can imagine my relationship not working in
> the very long term, but [I can't imagine] not being part of my children's life

The focus of our study and this book has sought to shift attention away
from families and the parent–child relationship so we will not further
interrogate the experience and meaningfulness of this 'bond'. Suffice to
say, it was perceived – as the above quotes illustrate – as foundational
and elemental: for mothers in particular, the most important of all relationships. Parenthood may put stress on the couple relationship (Walker
et al., 2010), as discussed in Chapter 4, but the decision to have a child
and its birth were typically perceived as positive points in the relationship
horizon, enshrining a sense of commitment to the couple project. As
Simmel argues, a dyad unit works only as long as both parties are committed to it. With the inclusion of a third party, the possibility of continuity emerges: there is life beyond both the individuals and the couple.
The arrival of a child adds another dimension, a third point that can
stabilise or cleave apart the two and that, as a result, may require different
or additional relationship work by the couple.

   In contrast to this expanding hub of intimacy for fathers and childfree couples there appeared to be a greater and single investment in the
partner and thus, by default, the dyadic unit. Participants who chose
their partner when asked who the most important person in their life
was framed this in terms of mutuality and embedded lives (Smart, 2007):
their partner gave meaning to their own life. These sentiments share,
therefore, a similar vernacular to those representing children. Participants
mentioned shared experiences – how, having gone 'through thick and
thin' and survived 'ups and downs' a stronger couple connection had
been forged. A partner was thus described as being their 'other half', an

'extension' of themselves. This close relationship created an intimate private world that was sustained by and through the couple.

> Because she is literally my other half. I have lived with her over half my life
> After 5 years together, with so much love and affection shared and so many in-jokes, routines, experiences, etc., it just feels like we have created our own private universe. It's hard to think of anything (or anyone) beyond that universe, which is the great constant in my life

Perhaps unsurprisingly few survey respondents mentioned anyone other than child or partner to the question about who the most important person in their life was. For childfree participants some did include family members, friends and self (as discussed in Chapter a), but these answers were negligible in terms of response rates to those of partner and child. In the qualitative data, however, some of these other affinities took on far more salience in terms of everyday living and/or comprising the underlying fabric of couple relationships. Pets, for example, often appeared as a crucial component in the relationship dynamic, being talked about with terms of sincere endearment.

Pets

For childfree couples, where children had left home or where parenthood did not feature, pets might be woven into the couple narrative. In some accounts, they appeared to stand in for children, but at other times they were valued as something more than this. In these instances pets were positioned as an integral part of the couple relationship, providing an attentive and listening ear, and symbolising and creating a sense of home.

ESTHER: Oh, we can't have a house without a pet in it [... Without a pet, a home] well, it's empty. It's empty isn't it?

ALAN: Um, it's part of the family, an animal. To me it is. Always has been.

ESTHER: Oh yeah, and you can tell them things you wouldn't tell somebody else.

ALAN: Yeah, you can talk to them [...]
ESTHER: you know, they'll sit at your feet but you can talk to them. They
             don't tell secrets and things like that.
ALAN: That's right, they don't.

For Esther and Alan, then, pets provide a willing repository for confidences; a safe space to test out feelings and vocalise what might otherwise be hard to say. In this sense, they serve as both mediator and facilitator in their relationship and are equally cherished by both partners. Here, as elsewhere, gendered stereotypes that associate men with emotional reticence and/or a lack of sentiment begin to unravel. Alan and Esther both confide in animals and respect the role that these creatures play in sustaining their couple relationship. Another participant identified her male partner as having the primary attachment to their pet.

EMMA: I think [partner] cares a lot about the hamster [laughs], kind of
             maybe more so than I do, I didn't expect him to sort of take
             such a liking to him [...] we do care about him a lot, he's been
             with me for two and a half years now, so, so yeah I guess he's
             become sort of part of my life, and I love animals. I mean I
             used to have rabbits and I grew up with dogs [...] I was really
             upset the other day, I can't remember why, but I just [... part-
             ner] was like, 'Oh, let's get the hamster out, come on', and you
             know, we got him out and had a play and just like holding him
             in my hands made me, just sort of really relaxed [me ...] having
             a pet, and I guess [partner] gets it too because he loves him so
             much, and, playing with him together kind of, we talk to him
             in silly voices and [laughs], and I guess maybe we bond with
             him, you know, like me and [partner] bond, by playing with
             our pet maybe.

Here we can see how pets are experienced as a source of comfort and affection for the individual and facilitate partnership attachment by providing a focal point through which past, present and future lives can be brought together. As Emma says, they have been a constant in her childhood and in adulthood alike and she appears to rely on the solace they can provide. In the present day, within the fabric of this couple relationship, caring for a pet is a form of relationship work, helping to bond the couple together through memories, newly crafted. In such circumstances, pets serve to consolidate the longevity of the relationship by their presence across the passage of time and through their capacity to help the couple through good and bad times, together.

For people who are not animal-focused, the claim that pets are part of a relationship seems incredulous. However, an estimated 53 per cent of British households own at least one pet (Pet Food Manufacturers Association (PFMA), 2003), including dogs, cats, rabbits, gerbils, fish, reptiles and a wide range of other creatures. The value of cross-species relationships in these household contexts is unquestionable (Gabb, 2011a). Research has situated pets in the 'liminal space' between animals and humans (Fox, 2008), identifying them as integral significant others in networks of extended or surrogate kin (Bonas, McNicholas, & Collins, 2000; Charles, 2014; Charles & Davies, 2008; Mason & Tipper, 2008). The work of Donna Haraway (2003, 2008) is particularly useful in unpicking the sociological meanings of human–animal relations and how these redraw the boundaries around kin, intimacy and intimates. Haraway takes issue with affective distinctions that are upheld through a scientific account of species identity (Robert & Baylis, 2003). For her, dogs are part of a 'queer family of companion species' (Haraway, 2003, p. 11). She moves beyond like kin and/or intimacy deficit models, wherein pets fulfil human needs, and situates human–animal ties within the context of wider networks of relationality. There is plentiful research evidence to support this line of thinking in the data from couples where pets featured as part of their household. For Ella and Russell, for example, their dog was an integral part of their 'kin-pack'. They acknowledged that this interpretation of 'unconditional love' was anthropomorphising, projecting their feelings onto another species. Nevertheless, in the process, this semantic realignment facilitated *their* inclusion of the dog within the couple relationship, invoking remarkably similar discourses to those evident in the previous section on the parent–child bond.

ELLA: [Dog's] just part of the family really. She's not quite 'our baby'
           [laughs] but if any of the animals were going to be, [the dog]
           would be it wouldn't it?

RUSSELL: Yeah [dog's] a bit of a distraction, a bit of fun, unconditional
           love coming back from her isn't it.

For younger couples, decision-making around family planning seemed
to position a child or a pet as almost interchangeable. Here, and in other
responses from participants in the younger age ranges, there was a ten-
dency to include animals as part of the couple's imagined family, all
together.

MONA: I think it would be a good thing whether we had children or
           whether we had a dog [...] Obviously there's going to be issues,
           there always is, because I watch my brother and watch my
           mates have kids and there's, you're so tired because you've got
           to stay up with the puppy or the baby and you're bereft of
           sleep, and you just find the inner strength and you sort of, you
           have to rely on each other a lot more, with a lot less patience I
           guess with everything [...] There would be challenges but it
           would be a positive, definitely a positive.

The gravitas of the decision to commit to a life project that would include
a dependant (child or pet) included an element of playfulness. The future
relationship, involving a lifelong commitment and associated responsibility, was almost beyond serious imagination *at this point in time*. Airing
such thoughts through discussion of pets appeared to enable some participants, such as Mona, to test out how future plans might map out,
including the impact of such dependants on the durability of the couple
relationship. In other accounts, pets seemed to provide a means through
which couples' impasse around family planning decisions could be bro-
kered and/or decisions fended off until another day when the timing
perhaps feels better. In these circumstances a pet was often positioned
as a substitute child and/or a means of addressing this seemingly intractable problem in the couple relationship. Pets thus featured in distinctive
ways, meeting different needs in a wide range of couple relationships,

and in these different scenarios they added another dimension to the couple dyad. In other scenarios it was not, however, a third party which unsettled the couple relationship. In these contexts, the dyadic unit in and of itself had little or no purchase.

Cultural difference

The specificity of cultural context remained crucial in shaping all couple relationships, whether explicitly acknowledged or tacitly taken for granted. For Prakash and his partner, a South Asian Gujarati couple, their accounts depict a contented and settled family life. They live with one of their sons, daughter-in-law and two young granddaughters. In their emotion maps they included no sign of couple intimacy. No space was designated private; indeed, as Figure 5.1 (below) illustrates, they ordinarily share their bed with the grandchildren. These data raise important issues for the *Enduring Love?* study about how we research and understand couple relationships more widely (Gabb & Singh, 2014).

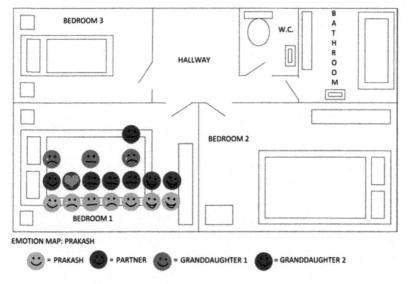

Figure 5.1   Prakash's emotion map

The presumption of intimacy and the intimate dyadic couple is called into question and perhaps – arguably – represents the wrong starting point for critical inquiry. The conjugal pairing that comprises the pro-creative sexual family (Fineman, 1995) does not reflect the experience of all couples in Britain today, if indeed it ever did (Davidoff et al., 1999). For Prakash and his partner, their couple relationship is so steeped in cultural expectations of intergenerational extended family care that contemporary western understandings of the intimate couple are rendered meaningless.

Prakash and his partner seldom experience their lives as 'a couple' and, when pushed on this point in interview, they expressed little or no interest in private couple time. When asked if they ever spent time alone together, they replied that they sometimes went to the supermarket together (Gabb & Singh, 2014). In response to the collage which depicted images of close embodied affection and sexual intimacy, the couple addressed their understandings of intimacy within their cultural purview and at their particular time in life, as an older couple, mentioning hugs and massage as important for their relationship.

Intimacy for this couple therefore is not defined through either sex or the proximity of two bodies alone. There is great fondness and physical affection between Prakash and his partner but their relationship does not revolve around understandings and expectations of intimacy that were typical in most other couples in the sample. Moreover, their relationship is markedly different from the cultural representations of being a couple that are portrayed in western culture. In this patriarchal extended family, it is expected that adult sons will live with their ageing parents, wherein the grandmother takes an active role in running the household and looking after the children. Indeed, preserving harmonious relationships with in-laws and valuing family relationships is fundamental in this couple's Indian culture (Kakar, 1981; Nath & Craig, 1999). These data, like those in Chapter 3, thus pose a critical reminder that western ideas of 'the couple' are not ubiquitous: couple relationships remain culturally specific. For example, while his partner's primary relationship seems to be with her grandchildren, for Prakash, notwithstanding his evident respect and fondness for his partner, his primary relationship appears to be with his God. For him and other couples where faith significantly shaped the meanings and experience of their couple relationships, deities played a crucial role and serve to consolidate the dyadic partnership.

In survey responses to the open question 'What do you like best about your relationship?', issues of sharing featured very prominently with particular emphasis being placed on sharing values, a faith, beliefs, tastes, ambitions and interests with their partner (Gabb et al., 2013). Men's answers rated this item in first place in the things they liked best about their relationship, while the responses of mothers and childfree participants placed it second.[4] Correspondingly, the lack of a shared faith or different political views was cited in answers to the companion question 'What do you like least about your relationship?'[5] Participants expressed their sense of unease around substantive differences, mentioning how their struggle to accommodate a partner's opposing beliefs and values adversely affected their relationship. In the qualitative data, for those couples who were observant – that is to say, where faith informed both beliefs and their everyday practices – scriptures and doctrinal teachings provided a template and highly valued source of sustenance for their long-term relationship.

THOMAS: Marriage is, you know, yeah, 'til death do us part' [...] it's hard, you have to work hard at it because there's, there's lots of temptation out there and stuff and when times are difficult and you're going through difficult times on things. We're fortunate because we believe the same stuff, God is at the core of my life and [partner]'s life so it's, you know, the biggest core, common element [...]

CHRISTY: From our faith perspective we believe there's a way things are meant to be done and that God has the ... the best way. The way that he thinks is the best for us.

Thomas and Christy understand what it means to *be* a couple through Christian Bible scriptures. There is a 'right' way to live together as a couple – and family – and they structure their married lives through these teachings. The underpinning impact of faith on how observant couples experienced and perceived their relationships was fundamental (Butler, Gardner, & Bird, 1998) and in these contexts, the adage that 'those who pray together stay together' was meaningful and real. The sharing of beliefs and commitment to the life-long relationship project has been associated with relationship quality and some research has shown a positive correlation between religiosity and relationship satisfaction (Lin & Huddleston-Casas, 2005; Mahoney, Pargament, Murray-Swank, & Murray-Swank, 2003). However, the perceptions of this cohort may be rated more positively because of a personal sense of responsibility, that is, their relationship is sanctified by God and therefore *has to be good*. There is not scope here to fully interrogate the ways that faith shaped different relationships and/or to address the question of relationship quality in these different contexts. Suffice to say that for couples like Christy and Thomas, the sacrament of marriage is foundational in shaping their lives. It enshrines their lifelong commitment to each and an open embrace of their God as the third party in their relationship.

CHRISTY: We believe that this God is the God that created everything and has the best for us, then the more we know of him, the more we know of what he wants us to do and where he wants us to go […] but ultimately God is never crowded because he is our focus […] as you grow closer to God, you grow closer to each other as well because God's ways are your ways then, because that relationship is so close that that's how it all works out together.

THOMAS: There's three of us with God [… but] it's not crowded at all, not crowded.

The relationship that Christy and Thomas went on to describe was expanded still further to include their children and their local church congregation. The form, composition and rules of this relationship were perceived as ultimately not theirs to determine. Their tripartite relationship was embraced because their God was involved in all dimensions of their everyday lives and informed the 'rules' that shaped the relationship. Whereas for Prakash and his partner the intimate couple and love are of secondary importance to family, for Christy and Thomas, their God *is* love and the sexual union must therefore be sustained in His name. To describe either of these couples as dyadic would misrepresent how they lived their lives, their relationship practices and their perception of what counts in their relationship.

Non-monogamies

While the analogy may seem paradoxical, there are marked similarities in the framing of the Christian relationship described in the previous section and those posed by other couples who described their relationships as open or non-monogamous. Four such couples took part in the qualitative dimension of our study and each of these couples identified as non-heterosexual (bisexual, gay and queer). It is important, however, not to conflate queer sexualities with non-traditional lifestyles. As we say at the outset of this chapter, our sampling frame was constituted through demographic factors; relationship rules such as these did not drive recruitment, and the inclusion of this dimension in our study provides anecdotal data that should not be identified as a defining characteristic of a particular group. The examples here serve as an illustration of another form of relationship configuration which pushes at the boundaries of the couple dyad.

In the context of open, non-monogamous and polyamorous relationships, the sexual was often relevant as a factor in shaping the relational dynamic. For Emmie and Theo, for example, sharing other sexual relationships was a fundamental part of their married life together. They perceived their marriage as simultaneously subversive because of its open nature and conventional in that it marked a deeply personal commitment to each other.

EMMIE: [The] important bit being that the rules stay the same for both of us, we can both have other partners but we have to be open and honest about it […] you see that in the relationship with [male lover], that's exactly what we do, it's that kind of openness, that kind of honesty and that is really at the heart of our relationship is that acceptance of, if we talk through things, if we don't hide anything from each other […] that gives us a solid foundation, that kind of trust [… that] sort of comfort zone in a sense. I know that I can go to Theo and there will always be something comfortable there, you know, whatever madness is going on around me, there's always comfort in his arms.

The couple relationship described here provides Emmie's primary intimacy and emotional security – her source of 'comfort'. But within this dyad there is also space for a mutual lover. This inclusion of a third party disrupts the couple dyad; as Emmie says, 'There's a kind of triangle between us.' Trust and openness shape this relationship and the couple are clearly 'rewriting the rules' (Barker, 2012) in ways that work, in practice, for them. Their rules may be transgressive and permissive but they are also clearly defined. Openness does not equate 'anything goes': on the contrary non-monogamy takes a lot of relationship work. Relationship practices which may appear small and inconsequential to the outside eye are steeped in meaning for this couple and, like those of Christy and Thomas, are crucial in sustaining their long-term relationship and marriage.

EMMIE: We have post-coital tea which is a separate thing. We have a particular two mugs, and I think [lover] … when he first came down here because he picked [my mug] up and I just went, 'Don't, don't use that mug.' [Laughing]

THEO: […] once we've had sex, we had a cup of tea, and Emmie usually makes it and we've got two, just two purple mugs that match, and we only use them for that purpose […] that's just a little, a little ceremony kind of thing […] you know, it just became part of our experience […] and as I say we made it, we formalised it and made it, gave it more meaning by having exclusive items for it and things like that.

Emmie and Theo's lover is thus simultaneously situated both inside and outside of the couple relationship. He adds something to it but the specialness and permanence of their couple relationship is distinct and precious. For another couple, Marico and his male partner, *their* relationship was less clearly defined. As a new lover was welcomed into their lives, their relationship boundaries were stretching beyond the primary dyad and they were working at building a triadic partnership that would include this lover within their intimate lives, all together (Figure 5.2).

MARICO: [Lover] fell asleep on the couch snuggled around [partner]. I then carried [lover] to bed, and we both kissed [him] good-night. That was a wonderful episode.

Later that night, I spent some time talking with [partner] about the events of the day to reflect on them and adapt communicative behaviour that might've led to unhappiness.

We then discussed who was going to sleep where (the bed in the bed-room is too small for the three of us).

[... Next day] After I had woken up, I had a shower. When I got out, [partner] had sent me a text that they were awake and I was free to join them in the bed/room. I did so, we cuddled a bit, and then had breakfast/lunch.

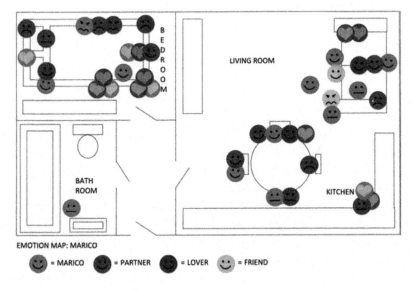

Figure 5.2 Marico's emotion map

In Marico's emotion map there is no clear-cut separation between new and old partners as they navigate their way around shifting emotional and spatial relationship boundaries. Again, openness and dialogue are crucial in this process. Ambivalent or anxious feelings are talked about, through different configurations of the partnership and via different modes of communication. Respect underpins these exchanges, both for the feelings experienced and around the need for privacy within openness. For example, Marico was invited into the bedroom which was being occupied by his partner and their lover. Open relationships are not effortless; they require significant relationship work. Whereas the couples discussed in Chapter 2 danced around the house to their favourite tunes or in elaborate strategies of avoidance, the partners here are choreographing triadic relationships that have developed their own emotional and spatial rhythms.

Friends

Participants' accounts of open and non-monogamous relationships were typically shaped by transparency and frank discussions of relationship boundaries. Extra-marital relationships were in many ways the antithesis of this openness; as we discussed in Chapter 3, they were often shrouded in secrecy and deception. Several of our couples disclosed how they or their partner had previously had an affair and most spoke about both the pain and rawness still experienced and how working through the sense of betrayal that accompanied these events eventually served to strengthen the couple relationship. During such times, the couple dyad may be locked down as private reparation work is completed; the outside word is kept at bay and potential intervention (and/or interference) fended off. However, before the emotional drawbridge is pulled up, other close friends and family members may be drawn in rather than kept out. These trusted individuals are called upon to provide the emotional care and sometimes the practical support to see the couple through such difficult periods. For example, Paul and Christine openly acknowledged how friends had challenged his behaviour following his extra-marital affair.

PAUL: And for me ... having an affair years back, and, significant for me during that period were friends; my friends that have a lot of regard for Christine [partner]that just said, 'Paul, what the fuck are you doing? Get your act together'. [...] so they were very significant for me then.

Christine spoke about the positive role played by friends more generally. She reflected that their long-term relationship had been sustained not only by their own input and energies, as a couple, but also by the emotional and practical input of friends and family. She queried whether they could have stayed together: 'If it was just on our own, who knows? Would we have done it?' Her rhetorical questions call out for reassurance and suggest the very positive contributions of friendship in their relationship. Together, then, they each acknowledge the role played by others who might ordinarily and discursively be situated outside the couple relationship, but whose presence and intervention was perceived as decisive. Here, and in other couples' accounts, friends and family are central in helping to build and hold together the couple relationship. Through such examples it is possible to see how couple relationships include, and are shaped through, wider intimate networks. The diversity of who and what matters in couple relationships – above and beyond the couple dyad – emerges as a clearer but more complicated picture.

Our findings illustrate the different ways in which participants drew on the intimacy, support and encouragement of others to maintain their relationships over the long term through good and bad times. They demonstrate how couple experiences are enriched by intimate and emotional interactions beyond the dyadic partnership. Indeed, friendships were often identified as crucial at critical points, providing the emotional and practical sustenance that a partner was otherwise unable to provide.

LEONA: Oh, [sighing], I turned to a friend whose dad had died a similar time to my dad but a few years before [...] he was a really big support to me because he felt very similar to the way that I felt. So he would talk to me about how he got through those things [...I'm] very much in need of the physical close support of somebody putting their arm round me, or of holding

> my hand and just being there. Not even saying anything, just being there with me so that I know that I've got someone [... Partner] he's just different. And, he probably sees that I'm completely and utterly different in some ways as well. And, you can't make somebody be everything you need them to be ... you can't be the perfect person and supply the other person with everything they need, it's absolutely impossible [... Partner] never showed any jealousy [...] to be honest I probably didn't think a lot about what [partner] thought about it, because I knew that he couldn't provide that for me at the time being honest [laughter].

It is suggested that friendships and shared confidences are particularly prevalent and valued among women (Pahl & Pevalin, 2005), and Leona's recourse to friendship to support her through this particularly difficult time certainly bears this out. But the silent voice here – that of her *male* friend – tells a different story. *He* also turned to her. Their friendship and shared confidences crossed the gender boundary and as such trouble the highly gendered account of friendship that is taken for granted both in the academy and across society more widely. Moreover, the friendship between Leona and this man ran alongside their respective couple relationships, dipping in and out as it was needed or wanted. Her partner was not threatened by it; indeed, in his individual and couple interview he expressed relief that someone took on this role that he felt ill-equipped to meet. This otherwise highly traditional couple, therefore, also serve to contest the idea of 'the one', wherein a partner is expected to meet our each and every need.

What separated the parties in Leona's account were sexual intimacy and the couple's commitment to marriage and monogamy. As we discussed in Chapter 3, friendship is commonly understood to be non-sexual and, conversely, sexual relationships are seen to have a different basis to those of friendship (Jamieson, 1998). However, in LGBQ networks the 'friendship ethic' is often said to blur the intimate boundaries (see Weeks et al., 2001, pp. 51–76), crafting a new elective family form which reflects 'an index of changing social possibilities and demands' (Weeks, 2000, p. 219) and requiring a queering of sociological thought

(Budgeon & Roseneil, 2004). Situating friendship as a lens through which to see all relationships is identified as 'key to understanding non-heterosexual ways of life' (Weeks et al., 2001, p. 51). It brings to light how queer networks of intimacy span the affective spectrum, including platonic friendships, ex-lovers and current sexual partnerships.

Most of the LGBQ participants in our study were aware of the 'families of choice' discourse (Weeks et al., 2001; Weston, 1997) and many spoke openly about the value of friendships, often affording them a significant place in their couple narratives. Of those couples, where relationships were identified as non-monogamous, the boundaries between friendship and sexual partnership might be perceived as the most permeable. Joss and Jake, for example, both identify as bisexual and define their relationship as polyamorous. They talked about the importance of having individual friends as well as friends who are shared friends, and these friendships were carefully woven into the fabric of their family lives. This did not mean that partners beyond the couple were simply introduced to children, but neither were they kept outside of the household.

Joss: When I was seeing [ex-girl/friend] quite regularly, I think [son] picked something up that [she] was in a different category from mummy's other friends [...] I think he had [her] in a different category in his head from my other friends.

Joss went on to talk about how being queer makes her more attuned to the politics around relationships and friendship and, as such, how she perceives herself to be highly reflexive. Indeed, Joss and Jake are evidently practising a high level of reflexivity in terms of how they live their lives and negotiate their polyrelationship.

Couple display

In their couple interview, Joss and her partner Jake described how their sexuality politics were crucial in shaping their private lives. As part of their personal–political identities, they were engaged in forms of relationship work that actively resisted any compulsion to be identified as a couple. Being conjoined in this way made them feel uneasy, undermining their sense of being individuals in their own right.

JOSS:	I don't particularly, don't like it if we're in a situation where I'm there as your partner. It happened the other day … when you were playing your cricket match and you were introducing me to people as your partner and I was all –
JAKE:	Oh yes. Yes, yes, that felt really weird actually. Yes, that was strange.
JOSS:	I didn't like that. I don't like being there as your appendage.
JAKE:	No, no, no.
JOSS:	And … a couple of [friends'] barbecues that we've been to. I really didn't like those, yes and that was partly about just being there as your partner.

For Joss and Jake, therefore, managing the public–private boundaries of their relationship requires considerable and consistent work. For LGBQ couples in the *Enduring Love?* study, deciding how, when or whether to display their relationship was often a source of discussion and negotiation, and there was no identifiable consensus across the dataset. The International Lesbian, Gay, Bisexual, Trans and Intersex Association (ILGA, 2014) has identified the UK as one of the most progressive countries for lesbian and gay rights, and UK social attitudinal data indicate growing tolerance of lesbian and gay relationships (Duncan & Phillips, 2008). Key legislative changes underpin and derive from these attitudinal shifts. Parenting opportunities have advanced through IVF (in vitro fertilisation) being made available for lone mothers (2005) and same-sex couples (2009). Lesbian and gay couples have been afforded legal recognition through civil partnership legislation (2005) and same-sex marriage (2014). The impact of these changes on couples who want to celebrate and claim legal recognition of their relationships remains significant. Parenting possibilities now feature in the imagined futures of LGBQ relationships. Whether or not to have children is now a decision that is ordinarily discussed and, for younger couples in particular in the study, it was the choices of 'when' and 'which way' to conceive that seemed to perplex them. However, caution should be exercised with claims made around the extent of these sexuality–parenting changes. While there is social acceptance of lesbian and gay couples and queer parenting more widely, the fear of reprisals or simply the fear of being stigmatised still featured as a prohibitive influence on the display of the couple relationships. Perhaps most surprisingly, this was expressed by younger couples in the cohort more than their older LBGQ counterparts.

BEX: I don't like to walk down the street holding Emma's hand. It's not that I'm bothered about what people think; it's more about am I putting us in danger by doing that. It's more of a protective thing, like I don't want to be physically or verbally abused as I'm walking down the street.

EMMA: Because it does always happen, when we're out and about. Not every time we're out and about … some people are cool with it but then there's other people who are like 'Yay, the entertainment's here' and we're like constantly watched, even if we're just having a meal or something. Everyone's like 'Oh my god, that's different'.

There may be widespread cultural shifts in ideas and experiences of family and recent inclusive legislation may have afforded parental rights and legitimacy to lesbian and gay couples in the eyes of the law, but, on the ground, heteronormative understandings of family are harder to destabilise, so too homophobia. The determining characteristic of parental roles remains 'hetero-gender' (Ingraham, 1996), being materialised through female/mother and male/father descriptors that map onto women and men. The significance of *recognition* (Finch, 2007) is crucial, but the display of particular relationships and/or identities remains tightly scrutinised (Gabb, 2013) and not all recognisable displays receive affirming receptions (Gabb, 2011b). The depressing regularity of brutal and sometimes fatal homophobic attacks, on gay men in particular, suggests that the impact of legislation and professed advances in social tolerance of LGBQ sexuality are not wholesale. Public spaces can be sites of high risk for those who display their homosexuality.

Public censorship of the couple relationship, therefore, is something negotiated and agreed upon within the individual couple relationship. For

Bex and Emma, their couple status is strategically displayed. For others, like Joss and Jake, it is personally and *politically* important not to be identified as a couple in public. For other LGBQ participants such as Marico, publicly displaying his triadic relationship is part of his queer identity. Such display suggests a heart-felt emotional need for his relationship and lifestyle to be socially recognised. The spectacle of the three men holding hands is thus designed to serve a political purpose in that it confronts heteronormative understandings of what partnerships can be. It knowingly requires members of the general public to question their taken-for-granted attitudes.

MARICO: [Partner] and [lover] were very nice to me and made tea [...] We then went on a long walk through [city in southern England], variably holding hands (mostly all three of us together), kissing, etc. People often looked at us puzzled, but we didn't mind them – or much rather enjoyed that we were unsettling traditional ideas about relationships.

This need for recognition of their relationship is not exhibitionism, although there is a sense of enjoying the shock value of the public display of their difference. It is also deeply personal for these men to capture touching moments within their relationship. Both men talked about their emotional investment in photographs taken which feature the three men and positively portray their shared intimacy. These images are not simply visual mementoes or keepsakes; they are a way of reinforcing the relational dynamic. The public and private display of their relationship thus validates the relationship externally and internally, between the partners.

Findings from the *Enduring Love?* study suggest that understandings of 'the couple' fail to recognise the diversity of relationship practices which feature across the intimate spectrum. Current relationship research and commentary on non-dyadic partnerships and non-monogamies ordinarily position other parties through 'the sexual', focusing on open relationships and elicit affairs. In our analysis here, however, we have demonstrated that what constitutes couple (dyadic) relationships and their slippage into, and conflation with, cultural understandings of the western heteronormative 'couple norm' cannot be taken for granted. The absence or presence of sex is not *the* defining component in shaping relationship parameters: our findings call into question boundaries and binaries often without recourse to sex. Relationships come in all shapes and sizes, forms and ephemera, and manifest across species. Couple relationships are not contained in the dyadic. The queer critique of coupledom is right to point to the privileges afforded to 'the couple' in contemporary cultural discourses and social policies; however, in so doing, it instantiates the very object that it sets out to question. In this chapter and in the book more widely, we have demonstrated that there is no unitary couple or shared sense of coupledom. Diversity and triadic configurations mark couples' embedded lives. The 'charmed circle' (Rubin, 1984) is indeed expanded and expansive, but not simply as an ideological means to reinforce a doctrine of compulsory coupledom. Instead, our focus on 'the everyday' has shown the richness of couple practices of intimacy and the diversity of the networks of support, companionship and intimacy which constitute and sustain them. All of these relational configurations now occupy and enrich the dynamic, enchanted sphere of couple relationships.

Notes

1. See Appendix 1 for sampling details.
2. See Appendix 2, Table A2.4: 'Who is the most important person in your life?' Gender and parenthood by age of youngest child.
3. See Appendix 2, Table A2.8: Means and Standard Deviations for relationship measures by gender and parenting status.
4. See Appendix 2, Table A2.2: 'What do you like best about your relationship?'
5. See Appendix 2, Table A2.3: 'What do you like least about your relationship?'

References

Barker, M. (2012). *Rewriting the Rules*. London: Routledge.
Barker, M., & Langdridge, D. (2010). Whatever Happened to Non-monogamies? Critical Reflections on Recent Research and Theory. *Sexualities, 13*(6), 748–772.

Bauman, Z. (2003). *Liquid Love: On the Frailty of Human Bonds*. Cambridge: Polity Press.

Beck, U. (2000). Living Your Own Life in a Runaway World: Individualization, Globalization and Politics. In W. Hutton & A. Giddens (Eds.), *On the Edge: Living with Global Capitalism* (pp. 164–174). London: Cape.

Beck, U., & Beck-Gernsheim, E. (1995). *The Normal Chaos of Love*. Cambridge: Polity Press.

Bonas, S., McNicholas, J., & Collins, G. (2000). Pets in the Network of Family Relationships: An Empirical Study. In A. Podberscek, E. Paul, & J. Serpell (Eds.), *Companion Animals and Us* (pp. 209–236). Cambridge: Cambridge University Press.

Budgeon, S. (2008). Couple Culture and the Production of Singleness. *Sexualities, 11*(3), 301–316.

Budgeon, S., & Roseneil, S. (2004). Editors' Introduction: Beyond the Conventional Family. *Current Sociology, 52*(2), 127–134.

Butler, M. H., Gardner, B. C., & Bird, M. H. (1998). Not Just a Time-Out: Change Dynamics of Prayer for Religious Couples in Conflict Situations. *Family Process, 37*(4), 451–478.

Charles, N. (2014). 'Animals Just Love You as You Are': Experiencing Kinship across the Species Barrier. *Sociology, 48*(4), 715–730.

Charles, N. & Davies, C. A. (2008). My Family and Other Animals: Pets as Kin. *Sociological Research Online, 13*(5). Retrieved from http://www.socresonline.org.uk/13/15/14.html

Coser, L. A. (1977). *Masters of Sociological Thought: Ideas in Historical and Social Context*. New York: Harcourt Brace Jovanovich.

Davidoff, L., Doolittle, M., Fink, J., & Holden, K. (1999). *The Family Story: Blood, Contract and Intimacy, 1830–1960*. London: Longman.

Duncan, S., & Phillips, M. (2008). New Families? Tradition and Change in Modern Relationships. In A. Park, J. Curtice, K. Thomson, M. Phillips, M. Johnson, & E. Clery (Eds.), *British Social Attitudes: The 24th Report*. London: Sage.

Finch, J. (2007). Displaying Families. *Sociology, 41*(1), 65–81.

Fineman, M. A. (1995). *The Neutered Mother, the Sexual Family, and Other Twentieth Century Tragedies*. New York: Routledge.

Fox, R. (2008). Animal Behaviour, Post-Human Lives: Everyday Negotiations of the Animal-Human Divide in Pet-Keeping. *Social & Cultural Geography, 7*(4), 525–537.

Gabb, J. (2008). *Researching Intimacy in Families*. Basingstoke: Palgrave Macmillan.

Gabb, J. (2011a). Family Lives and Relational Living: Taking Account of Otherness. *Sociological Research Online, 16*(4). Retrieved from http://www.socresonline.org.uk/16/14/10.html

Gabb, J. (2011b). Troubling Displays: The Affect of Gender, Sexuality and Class. In E. Dermott & J. Seymour (Eds.), *Displaying Families: A New Concept for the Sociology of Family Life* (pp. 38–60). Basingstoke: Palgrave Macmillan.

Gabb, J. (2013). Embodying Risk: Managing Father–Child Intimacy and the Display of Nudity in Families. *Sociology, 47*(4), 639–654.

Gabb, J., Klett-Davies, M., Fink, J., & Thomae, M. (2013). *Enduring Love? Couple Relationships in the 21st Century. Survey Findings Report*. Milton Keynes: The Open University. Retrieved from http://www.open.ac.uk/researchprojects/enduringlove/files/enduringlove/file/ecms/web-content/Final-Enduring-Love-Survey-Report.pdf.

Gabb, J., & Singh, R. (2014). Reflections on the Challenges of Understanding Racial, Cultural and Sexual Differences in Couple Relationship Research. *Journal of Family Therapy.* doi:10.1111/1467-6427.12044.

Giddens, A. (1992). *The Transformation of Intimacy: Sexuality, Love and Eroticism in Modern Societies*. Cambridge: Polity Press.

Haraway, D. (2003). *Companion Species Manifesto: Dogs, People, and Significant Otherness*. Chicago: Prickly Paradigm Press.

Haraway, D. (2008). *When Species Meet*. Minneapolis: University of Minnesota Press.

ILGA. (2014). Rainbow Europe. What Is It Like to Be Lesbian, Gay, Bisexual, Trans and Intersex in Europe? Retrieved 29 October 2014, from http://www.ilga-europe.org/home/publications/reports_and_other_materials/rainbow_europe

Ingraham, C. (1996). The Heterosexual Imaginary. Feminist Sociology and Theories of Gender. In S. Seidman (Ed.), *Queer Theory/Sociology* (pp. 168–193). Cambridge, MA: Blackwell.

Jamieson, L. (1998). *Intimacy: Personal Relationships in Modern Societies*. Cambridge: Polity Press.

Jamieson, L. (1999). Intimacy Transformed? A Critical Look at the 'Pure' Relationship. *Sociology, 33*(3), 477–494.

Jamieson, L. (2011). Intimacy as a Concept: Explaining Social Change in the Context of Globalisation or Another Form of Ethnocentricism? *Sociological Research Online, 16*(4). Retrieved from http://www.socresonline.org.uk/16/14/15.html

Jamieson, L., Morgan, D., Crow, G., & Allan, G. (2006). Friends, Neighbours and Distant Partners: Extending or Decentring Family Relationships?

Sociological Research Online, 11(3). Retrieved from http://www.socresonline. org.uk/11/13/jamieson.html

Kakar, S. (1981). *The Inner World. A Psycho-analytic Study of Childhood and Society in India.* Delhi: Oxford University Press.

Lin, L. W., & Huddleston-Casas, C. A. (2005). Agape Love in Couple Relationships. *Marriage & Family Review, 37*(4), 29–48.

Mahoney, A., Pargament, K. I., Murray-Swank, A., & Murray-Swank, N. (2003). Religion and the Sanctification of Family Relationships. *Review of Religious Research, 44*(3), 220–236.

Mason, J. (2008). Tangible Affinities and the Real Life Fascination of Kinship. *Sociology, 42*(1), 29–45.

Mason, J., & Tipper, B. (2008). Being Related. How Children Define and Create Kinship. *Childhood, 15*(4), 441–460.

Morgan, D. H. J. (1996). *Family Connections: An Introduction to Family Studies.* Cambridge: Polity Press.

Nath, R., & Craig, J. (1999). Practising Family Therapy in India: How Many People Are There in a Marital Subsystem? *Journal of Family Therapy, 21*, 390–406.

Pahl, R., & Pevalin, D. (2005). Between Family and Friends: A Longitudinal Study of Friendship Choice. *British Journal of Sociology, 56*(3), 433–450.

PFMA. (2003). *Pet Ownership, Pet Population Trends, Facts and Figures.* Retrieved 5 October 2013, from http://www.pfma.com/petownershipstats.html

Rich, A. (1980). Compulsory Heterosexuality and Lesbian Existence. *Signs, 5*(4), 631–660.

Robert, J., & Baylis, F. (2003). Crossing Species Boundaries. *The American Journal of Bioethics, 3*(3), 1–13.

Roseneil, S. (2000). Queer Frameworks and Queer Tendencies: Towards an Understanding of Postmodern Transformations of Sexuality. *Sociological Research Online, 5*(3). Retrieved from www.socresonline.org.uk/5/3/roseneil. html

Roseneil, S., & Budgeon, S. (2004). Cultures of Intimacy and Care beyond 'the Family': Personal Life and Social Change in the Early 21st Century. *Current Sociology, 52*(2), 135–159.

Rubin, G. (1984). Thinking Sex: Notes for a Radical Theory of the Politics of Sexuality. In C. Vance (Ed.), *Pleasure and Danger: Exploring Female Sexuality.* London: Pandora Press.

Simmel, G. (2012 [1908]). The Dyad and the Triad (from *The Sociology of Georg Simmel*). In C. Calhoun, J. Gerteis, & J. Moody (Eds.), *Classical Sociological Theory.* Chichester, West Sussex: Wiley-Blackwell.

Smart, C. (2007). *Personal Life*. Cambridge: Polity Press.

Smith, A. M. (2007). *Welfare Reform and Sexual Regulation*. Cambridge: Cambridge University Press.

Stacey, J. (2011). *Unhitched: Love, Marriage, and Family Values from West Hollywood to Western China*. New York: New York University Press.

Walker, J., Barrett, H., Wilson, G., & Chang, Y.-S. (2010). *Understanding the Needs of Adults (Particularly Parents) Regarding Relationship Support. Research Brief DCSF-RBX-10-01*. London: DCFS.

Weeks, J. (2000). *Making Sexual History*. Cambridge: Polity Press.

Weeks, J., Donovan, C., & Heaphy, B. (1999). Everyday Experiments: Narratives of Non-Heterosexual Relationships. In E. B. Silva & C. Smart (Eds.), *The New Family?* (pp. 83–99). London: Sage.

Weeks, J., Heaphy, B., & Donovan, C. (2001). *Same Sex Intimacies: Families of Choice and Other Life Experiments*. New York: Routledge.

Weston, K. (1997). *Families We Choose. Lesbians, Gays, Kinship*. New York: Columbia University Press.

Wilkinson, E. (2013). Learning to Love Again: 'Brosken Families', Citizenship and the State Promotion of Coupledom. *Geoforum, 49*, 206–213.

Williams, F. (2004). *Rethinking Families. Moral Tales of Parenting and Step-Parenting*. London: Calouste Gulbenkian Foundation.

6

Conclusion

Our analysis throughout this book has been shaped by a practices approach because, as we maintained in Chapter 1, it usefully moves the focus away from a structural analysis of relationship forms and opens up the diverse sets of interactions through which couples understand and experience their lives together. In this concluding chapter, we want to emphasise further the value of relationship practices as a conceptual framework for the study of long-term couple relationships by arguing that they highlight both the dynamics of these relationships and the significance of the spatio-temporal contexts in which they are situated. We thus weave a differently textured pattern in this chapter out of the themes that earlier chapters have addressed in order to reinforce three major findings from the *Enduring Love?* study and illustrate how these offer fresh understandings of the ways couples live and love in contemporary Britain.

© The Author(s) 2018
J. Gabb, J. Fink, *Couple Relationships in the 21st Century*, Palgrave Macmillan Studies in Family and Intimate Life, DOI 10.1007/978-3-319-59698-3_6

Time and the mundane nature of relationship work

First, we would suggest that the study opens up new insights into the relationship work that couples undertake to sustain their lives together and, more particularly, the nature of relationship practices that comprise such work. Relationships practices are central to how couple relationships are experienced and given meaning at the level of the everyday and they require an investment of time in all its different dimensions (Adams, 2004). This is not because such practices are necessarily demanding time-wise in and of themselves; as we have emphasised in each chapter, the most cherished acts and gestures are often comprised of minutiae and mundanities. It is rather that their value lies in the time and care habitually devoted to them. The thoughtful gesture of bringing a partner a cup of tea in bed builds into meaningful relationship work when it is undertaken as a regular, everyday practice. Similarly, the time invested in sharing commonplace activities, such as doing the shopping, is often appreciated because it routinely reconnects couples as we illustrated in Chapter 2. Where busy work schedules and/or the demands of childcare are all-pervading aspects of couples' daily lives, the loss of these small moments of time together is frequently mourned. Even the commute to work was described in one participant's diary as a welcome chance to spend some treasured time with her partner that would be missed when they no longer travelled together.

TAMSIV: Can't believe we've only got 4 weeks of travelling together [because of my impending maternity leave] … seems a bit sad and scary at the same time. Sad that we won't get to spend that 35 minutes together (even though we don't really talk).

It is perhaps not surprising, then, that our findings reveal how, for instance, couples take particular care to protect the time they have committed to jointly watching a TV series or DVD box set, or find genuine pleasure in unexpected opportunities in which to dance together or snatch a quick cuddle away from their children. Spending time together through such mundane relationship practices was perceived as enormously important by couples in the study; it was a connector not only *in* their relationship but it also added an emotionally meaningful dimension to the way they worked *on* their relationship.

However, couples also acknowledged the importance of taking 'time out' from a relationship and recognised the difficulties that could result when one partner needed to claim more personal space and the other was reluctant about such a shift in the relationship dynamic. As a relationship practice, having time away from one's partner is valued and appreciated by women and men alike because it generates a sense of independence and agency as well as opportunities to pursue personal interests or spend time with friends alone. It also works to dissipate conflict when, like Ria, one partner feels overwhelmed by the couple relationship and longs for more time apart.

RIA: It's not easy to tell the person that you love that you want to spend more time away from them and that when they get closer to you, you feel like punching them in the face [laughs]. It was really hard and it must have been really hard for her to swallow but she dealt with it so well. I mean she was angry for about five minutes and then after that she was just ... she just said, 'Well if that's what you need, that's what you need and that's what we'll do'.

Relationship work demands, therefore, a careful balancing of sharing time together, and establishing ways of spending time together apart or apart. Mundane relationship practices provide couples with resources to manage this potential tension in their lives, albeit that it may never be entirely resolved. Nevertheless, reflecting on what a partner might appreciate to make the humdrum nature of life more agreeable, sharing pleasurable moments at the end of a long day or accepting that 'togetherness' has to be mediated are all crucial elements in the ways couples work at their relationship – work that requires an investment of time both in the moment and over the life course. Barbara Adams has argued that 'economic time values' – where time is money and so faster is better – are now the norm in a globalised world of work. As a result, a great majority of people 'inhabit the shadowlands of un- and undervalued time (... where) their work is not accorded value in the capitalist scheme of things' (Adams, 2006, p. 124). Couples' relationship work might also be understood as 'unproductive work', not least because the time it requires would not be understood, in socio-economic terms, as having any monetary value. Yet the time that couples commit to working at their relationships – in the short, medium and long term – is arguably *in*valuable because it is only through such work that couples are able to build an intimate knowledge of each other and establish ways of sustaining their lives together. With the annual cost of family breakdown running at an estimated £44 billion (CSJ, 2014), as we noted in Chapter 1, it is clear that time invested by couples in work that nurtures and maintains their relationships does have a significant financial value and that understandings of the affective significance of such everyday humdrum work has, therefore, the potential to be productively integrated into relationship and family support services.

The meanings of love in contemporary times

The second strand in our findings that we want to emphasise here is the many and varied ways through which couples express their love for each other, day in and day out. However, doing and feeling love were often inextricably woven together in couples' accounts of their everyday lives and it could be equally difficult to disentangle how ideas about romantic, companionate and parental love were used by couples to explain what it means to love and be loved in contemporary times. Again, the idea of relationship practices was a crucial analytical lens for unpicking both the entangled meanings of love on which participants in our study drew, and the way these were embedded in routine banal activities as opposed to grand romantic gestures or overblown statements about undying devotion.

Relationship practices were repeatedly used by couples to say, show and enact their love for each other and to consolidate their sense of togetherness. 'I love you' was an expression often used by women in the study to communicate their feelings to a partner but words alone were also recognised as an insufficient demonstration of the intensity of attachment that one partner felt for the other. Acts of love and loving gestures are thus understood to be equally meaningful for a couple relationship and are valued because they implicitly convey feelings of love. Preparing a meal, for example, was regularly treated by men in our study as a loving gesture – a gesture that was received, equally, with love by their partner and recognition of the care and support it also represented.

DUNCAN: [Cooking] has evolved because of the work situation, and it's a nice feeling to know that if she had a bad day or a long day, whatever it is, and I'm able to make that a little bit easier, even if it's just having a cup of tea ready when she comes in, and things like that, so, you know, it's … yeah.

Such acts of love are one element of the many relationship practices that couples use to express their feelings for each other, as earlier chapters have argued, and to strengthen the emotional ties that join them together in the moment and over time. In this respect, perceived differences in the cultural imaginary between romantic and companionate love seem deeply problematic, as couples' accounts of their relating practices move constantly between the two, undermining the idea of any clear divide between the intensity of feeling and sexual energy in the former, and the congenial friendship of the latter. As we maintained in Chapter 4, in long-term relationships, sexual intimacy can be an opportunity for couples to express an ongoing passionate connection to each other – a connection that is not diminished by time, as often assumed, but rather enriched by the intimate knowledge accumulated over years spent together. Likewise, the importance of a sexual relationship does not overshadow or lessen the value placed on other dimensions of doing and feeling love. Zoe's explanation of her long-term relationship is one example of the way couples in the study negotiated and subverted the perceived boundaries between romantic and companionate love.

ZOE: That physical part of our relationship has always been like really, really important. It's the glue really that holds you together […] it's an essential part of who we are and who we are together and what drew us to be together and sustained us over the years as well [… but] the key thing as far as I see it is we're just incredibly good friends. I mean, you know, we're lovers as well and partners [...] we just really like each other and enjoy each other's company and have lots of [...] shared humour and shared kind of love of music and theatre and [...] arts and things [...] it's just an incredible kind of privilege to be with someone who you love that much.

The love that Zoe expresses for her partner is unambiguous but it cannot be easily defined. It is wrapped into the importance of their sexual relationship, the pleasures of time spent together and the sharing of interests and activities. It demands multiple terms to describe its depth and extent; the couple are simultaneously lovers, friends and partners and, as such, Zoe's interview is redolent of Maddie's collage in Chapter 3, albeit that as a childfree woman there is no mention of parental love. What she means by the love she feels 'privileged' to experience cannot, therefore, be contained by ideas of either romantic or companionate love. Her account is a synthesis of romantic feeling and fond affection, which is woven into the fabric of her life and, like other couples' accounts in the study, is expressed and enacted through diverse relationship practices. Attending to the complex and fluid ways in which couples express their love for each other offers, then, an opportunity to revisit popular discourses of love, romance and coupledom and their problematic premise of expecting romantic love to sustain and contain all our emotional and practical needs. Our findings thus complement the critique of coupledom we discussed in Chapter 5, not by suggesting that intimate democracy (Beck & Beck-Gersheim, 1995; Giddens, 1991) and a contemporary makeover of love (Evans, 2002; Field, 1995) have failed to refashion the affective playing field, but rather by arguing that relationship practices offer insights into what love might mean *in practice* for couples in long-term relationships.

Communication and the importance of home

As we have emphasised in the book's different chapters, the home can provide a safe and protective environment for some couples, allowing them to engage in a raft of relationship practices through which to 'work' at their relationship, sustain the emotional and physical intimacy of their lives together and create opportunities to craft and display diverse experiences of 'coupledom'. This final thread in our discussion of the study's findings takes the home as its focus in order to explore further its significance for understanding the possibilities for, and challenges of, communication in long-term couple relationships. Our discussion here does not presuppose that the spatial dimension of relationship practices is confined to the home (Morgan, 2011); rather, it is informed by the study's multiple methods which were predominantly focused on couples' experiences and feelings 'at home'.

Situating the home as an important dynamic in the ways that couples communicate with each other brings to the fore the triggers whereby conflict is sparked and more intimate connections are forged. One of the most intensely experienced sites of anger and exasperation in the home is around the gendered inequalities that shape responsibilities for domestic chores and childcare, and particularly when women are also trying to manage the 'double burden' of paid employment and the care of young children. In these situations parental leave and flexible working policies seem to offer little to address the difficulties of achieving an acceptable work–life balance and, moreover, the home is experienced as a space where feelings and experiences of unfairness coalesce and requests for support are left unheard.

Chapter 2 identified how some couples dance together and others dance around each other and also how these relationship practices bring into view the choices that couples make with regard to relating to each other. However, for some couples there is no space in the home to make such choices or opportunities to craft modes of communication that are specific to them and their needs, rather than the wider family unit. For Glen, a long-term unemployed young man, the chance of four weeks of paid work offered a way out of the home – a small housing association flat that he shared with his wife and two children – and all the tensions that ensue from spending too much time together in too small a space.

GLEN: I think [getting the job] will put an ease on [...] because we have [...] now and again got stressy with each other because we've been under each other's feet for a while, you know.

We've been there pretty much locked solid together, you know, and I'm not going to be doing that for the next four weeks, which, you know, will probably take the extra strain off.

Extended or extensive proximity, then, can be a significant factor in the breakdown of communication in couple relationships, particularly where other stressors such as unemployment and a lack of financial resources are involved. Yet for couples in more secure situations in life, the home is experienced as a very positive aspect of the ways they are able to share hopes, desires, needs and anxieties with each other. It provides a space to talk through events of the day, make plans for the future or reminisce about a past together. It holds the warmth and pleasure of knowing what a partner might be thinking, of sharing a joke together and of reflexively bickering about the inconsequentialities of everyday life. It also provides specific places where communication between couples can be best facilitated, whether this be cuddled up on the sofa, at the dining room table or, as Mary explains in her diary, in the bedroom.

MARY: 7.15am – as is our usual custom, [partner] brought me a cup of tea in bed. He has been up for some time. He has a shower in the ensuite and gets dressed while we chat about the news headlines on the radio and our plans for the day […] I really like this time with [partner]. When he is at home, he is not always relaxed, having a lot of nervous energy. This means that he will always find something to do in the house or the garden rather than just sitting and chilling out with me. However, in the mornings, as he is in the bedroom anyway getting ready for work, it comes naturally to have a dialogue – I don't get a sense that he feels he should be doing something else.

The home is, then, a fundamental dimension of couple relationships: a point of stability within the flux of couples' everyday lives together and a site where they can establish intimate connections with each other through diverse words, acts and gestures that combine to constitute their repertories of communication. Couples come together in the home emotionally, physically and practically, and build their sense of togetherness through relationship practices that are embedded not only in the fabric of its rooms and furniture but also in the ways 'home life' is imagined. Moreover, as we noted in Chapter 1, the importance of home in the emotional dynamics of couple relationships and in the practices through which they sustain their relationships can be usefully drawn into policy and practice debates about housing, relationship support and relationship education.

Conclusion

As we noted in the opening to this book, there has been much research on, and policy concern with, the breakdown of family life and the stressors which fracture long-term couple relationships. Through findings from the *Enduring Love?* study and our practices approach we have sought, therefore, to bring an obverse picture into view by focusing on what couples do to sustain their relationships while illustrating the importance of time and space to their practices. We acknowledge that the pressures exerted on relationships from factors such as bereavement, financial uncertainties, the birth of children, changes in employment and housing can stretch a couple to breaking point. However, our data suggest that these same stressors can also serve to consolidate relationships if couples have the necessary spatio-temporal, emotional and financial resources to negotiate them. Nevertheless, through the extraordinary and ordinary ups and downs of life together, there are evident differences in the gendered relationship work that women and men do together, in the ways that younger and older couples draw on relationship practices that befit particular points in the life course and in the opportunities that heterosexual and LGBQ couples have to display their relationships. These differences are shaped by social, political and cultural change, the life course rhythms of couple relationships and the everyday schedules through which couples organise their lives together. They are also shaped by the spaces and places in which these different temporal contexts of couple relationships are embedded and experienced.

We have thus endeavoured to resist a too neatly packaged analysis and conclusion to this book. Our methodology and interpretation of findings were designed to be fluid and attentive to complexity and change in order to capture the constantly shifting elements of couples' everyday lives. Our analytical lens has sought to retain the messiness of lived lives (Daly, 2003) because couple relationships are multidimensional in form, and resist uniform interpretation. Assumptions about the couple dyad and ideas of 'coupledom' are, we would maintain, impossible to uphold in the context of our findings. The tension and problematic for academic study as well as for policy and practice is, therefore, to hold the specificities of experience in concert with differences in couples' lived lives and the different practices through which they give meaning to, and sustain, their relationships together over time.

References

Adams, B. (2004). *Time*. Cambridge and Malden, MA: Polity Press.

Adams, B. (2006). Time. *Theory, Culture and Society, 23*(2–3), 119–138.

Beck, U., & Beck-Gernsheim, E. (1995). *The Normal Chaos of Love*. Cambridge: Polity Press.

CSJ. (2014). *Family Breakdown*. Retrieved 31 August 2014, from http://www.centreforsocialjustice.org.uk/policy/pathways-to-poverty/family-breakdown

Daly, K. J. (2003). Family Theory versus the Theories Families Live by. *Journal of Marriage and Family, 65*(4), 771–784.

Evans, M. (2002). *Love: An Unromantic Discussion*. Cambridge: Polity Press.

Field, N. (1995). *Over the Rainbow: Money, Class and Homophobia*. London: Pluto Press.

Giddens, A. (1991). *Modernity and Self-Identity: Self and Society in the Late Modern Age*. Cambridge: Polity Press.

Morgan, D. H. J. (2011). *Rethinking Family Practices*. Basingstoke: Palgrave Macmillan.

Appendix 1: Researching Couples' Long-Term Relationships

Researching couples' long-term relationships

This book is based on findings from our study *Enduring Love? Couple Relationships in the 21st Century*, which explored how couples experience, understand and sustain their long-term relationships. It was funded by the Economic and Social Research Council (ESRC RES-062-23-3056) and carried out between 2011 and 2013. At the core of the study's development was a commitment to ensuring not only its intellectual rigour but also its policy and practice relevance. We established, therefore, an advisory framework for the study which brought together leading academics and independent researchers in the field as well as policymakers and representatives from third sector organisations with key roles in providing relationship support and education. Their interest, contributions and interventions have been invaluable and illustrate how our dialogic approach was central to the success of the study's impact and public engagement.

In designing and implementing the study, we sought to situate emotions at the conceptual, methodological and analytical heart of our

© The Author(s) 2018
J. Gabb, J. Fink, *Couple Relationships in the 21st Century*, Palgrave Macmillan Studies in Family and Intimate Life, DOI 10.1007/978-3-319-59698-3

research inquiry as relationships are comprised of a whole spectrum of feelings and experiences. Our aim in this was to access the ways that everyday experience and emotions interact but also to ensure that we were able to portray vibrant and visceral accounts of long-term relationships. We thus sought to resist the deployment of relationship typologies that feature in some academic studies and relationship support services, focusing instead on research practices that would facilitate exploration of how sets of contexts, predispositions and lifestyles might combine in myriad ways to form and reform couple relationships. We also left open the definition of what might constitute a long-term relationship in order to better understand how couples themselves experienced and imagined their relationship as an enduring one. To these ends, we deployed a mixed methods research design with qualitative methods being used to drill down into the embodied, lived experience of couples and a survey to generate a large-scale quantitative and qualitative dataset on couples' everyday relationship practices.

Participants who took part in the qualitative dimension of the study are identified by two pseudonyms: the first accompanies their individual data, the second their couple interview data. This is to ensure that assurances of confidentiality are honoured, with individual accounts being kept separate from those of the couple. Such assurances also mean that no biographical details about our participants can be provided in this outline of the *Enduring Love? study.* In some instances, however, couples spoke about sharing their data. In these circumstances we sometimes draw on 'couple data' from both partners to advance a particular analytical point. In the absence of dialogue and/or personal contact, quotations from survey participants remain anonymous.

Online survey

Our online survey was located on the study's website www.enduring-love.co.uk and implemented using the free online survey and questionnaire software *SurveyMonkey*. It was implemented over a 12-month period. Participants were recruited through features and news coverage of the research study posted on various online forums, newsletters and community group noticeboards, especially those clustered around parenting, relationship support and the student population of the institutional host (The Open University). As a recruitment strategy for the qualitative dimension of the study and to boost under-represented groups in the survey cohort, the survey questionnaire was also implemented in hard copy format among 'hard to reach' community groups and networks. The survey generated 5445 responses worldwide. However, since our analysis in this book is concerned with the particular personal, socio-economic and political contexts of couple relationships in mainland Britain, our focus is on data from the survey's UK cohort only. This comprised a convenience sample of 4494 respondents.

In order to access the survey online, participants were required to go to the study's website where detailed information on the scope and methodology of the research was provided, alongside frequently asked questions (FAQs) which were attentive to issues related to research ethics. The survey was designed so that only those participants who stated they were in a long-term couple relationship could go on to complete it. Details of the survey sample's composition can be found in Appendix 2, Table A2.9. Like other large-scale studies on relationship support, our participation rates included a gendered skew, higher than average educational qualifications and a predominantly white cohort (Walker et al., 2010).

The survey included three sets of multiple-choice statements, using Likert scale responses ranging from 1 to 5. These spoke to the structuring interests of the *Enduring Love?* study overall and enabled us to identify patterns in behaviour and the factors which appeared to signal relationship satisfaction. In analysing these data we devised scales of

- Relationship quality
- Relationship with partner
- Relationship maintenance
- Happiness with relationship/partner
- Happiness with life

Principal Component Analysis with Varimax Rotation was used to produce these five relationship measures. We computed basic descriptive statistics for demographic information. Multivariate Analyses of Variance

(MANOVA) and correlation analyses were used to address more complex research questions, facilitating examination of relationship satisfaction and the patterning of relationship experience (for full details of survey design and analytical strategy, see Gabb et al., 2013).

Examination of these relationship measures, however, falls outside the remit of this book and its concern with relationship practices. Instead, our analysis is focused on survey answers to multiple-choice questions and open, free-text questions, in which participants were asked to say what they liked and disliked about their relationship, and what their partner did that made them feel appreciated. These questions generated over 10,000 responses in total, all of which were systematically coded using a grounded theory approach. To facilitate mixed methods analysis, across the dataset, our quantitative and qualitative coding frames were consistent.

Qualitative design and methods

The *Enduring Love?* study also had a major qualitative dimension. Our qualitative research sample consisted of 50 couples: women (n = 54), men (n = 43) and other/queer (n = 3). It included couples across three age cohorts: 18–34, 35–54 and 55–65+, with equal numbers of couples with and without children. Purposive sampling was used to recruit these three primary groups, enabling us to interrogate the study's key analytical foci: gender, generation and parenthood. Our aim was not, however, to map relationship practices and gendered roles onto men and women but rather to examine the impact of socio-cultural norms, personal biographies and social differences on how women and men behave in relationships and how they perceive emotional ties. Similarly, the age cohorts were not included as a means to impose determining criteria about the meanings of relationships for older or younger couples. They were used to facilitate an analysis attentive to the significance of 'generation' for understanding how being situated in a particular historical period might shape couple relationships and experience of life course transitions (Fink & Gabb, 2014; Nilsen & Brannen, 2014).

Other areas of social diversity included education/socio-economic status, sexual orientation, race/ethnicity and religious belief. The final composition of the qualitative sample therefore comprised 30 per cent 'working class' (classified through education, employment and self-identification); 58 per cent either married or in a civil partnership; and 50 per cent with a religious belief, including several couples where faith was identified as a defining feature in their lives. Four couples described their relationships as non-monogamous or open. Two of the couples lived apart. While the sample was predominantly white/British (76 per cent), we employed targeted strategies to recruit Asian participants (n = 14) so that we could complete meaningful analysis of racial and cultural differences among a clearly identified sample subset (Gabb & Singh, 2014). Similar strategies were deployed around sexual diversity, with the sample comprising 30 per cent lesbian, gay, bisexual and queer participants. Queer is used here as a category of self-identity. We also recruited among the 'trans' population and the sample includes four participants from this group.

Recruitment among local community, parenting and family support groups as well as faith communities gave us access to 'hard to reach' groups such as socially disadvantaged and minority ethnic couples. Lesbian and gay couples were recruited through targeted online forums, local community groups and through snowballing techniques among personal networks. The research team comprised many different 'voices', with consultant researchers being appointed to boost this diversity. Our research strategy was built on the premise that 'insider knowledge' can sensitise a research project to the specificities of experience and, in so doing, provide situated insight (Gabb & Singh, 2014). In these contexts, a researcher's 'insider status' often served to literally and conceptually often open doors (Gabb, 2004), affording an epistemic privilege (Fuss, 1991) and facilitating rapport. However, even where personal lives and identities coincided, the researcher typically remained a 'trusted outsider' (Bucerius, 2013) to more than one group of participants. This status served to further enhance the research relationship as knowledge about feelings could be entrusted to a researcher while, at the same time, a 'professional' distance was maintained.

The study's qualitative interrogation of the minutiae and mundanities of couples' relationship practices was undertaken using a rich palette of qualitative methods: emotion maps, diaries, individual interviews and photo-elicitation interviews with couples. Combined, these methods were designed to interrogate how couples sustain their relationships over time and to identify cross-cutting patterns of relationship experience. The complexity of our research design meant that in most instances field-work was completed over a one- to three-month period, including, on average, three to four research meetings that, for the majority of couples, took place in the privacy of their home. For those participants located in socially disadvantaged communities, however, we adapted research procedures to accommodate their circumstances as required. In this context, multi-method fieldwork was typically conducted over two days, with individual and couple interviews being completed outside of the home, in community centre settings, cafes and on The Open University campus. This did not presuppose that those in such circumstances lacked key skills and resources (Evangelou, Coxon, Sylva, Smith, & Chan, 2013) but instead aimed to respect issues of privacy that may have arisen due to overcrowded households. It also acknowledged the desires and/or needs of some participants to maintain personal boundaries, particularly where related to the social and territorial stigma of poverty which, as Wacquant (2008) says, may spoil, shape and mediate personal lives and relationships.

The first two methods – emotion maps and diaries – were completed simultaneously over the course of one week. Emotion maps began with a sketch of the floor plan of the couple's home and were designed to generate data on participants' emotional geographies by situating interactions in the material environment of the home (Gabb, 2008; 2009). In LAT (living apart together) relationships, two floor plans were produced although it was the case that one of the households was used and/or perceived as the 'couple home', at least during this period of fieldwork. Participants were given sets of coloured emoticon stickers (denoting laughter, happiness, indifference, sadness, upset, grumpiness/anger and love/affection) to represent the different emotional interactions between everyone living in or visiting the home, including the participant, their partner, children, family, friends, pets, and so on. While most emoticons needed little explanation, participants were advised that the heart sticker could encompass any loving act, gesture or feeling, from a friendly cuddle to sex (Figure A1.1).

Diaries aimed to generate temporal data on a couple's everyday routines but, with their status as a 'confessional' device (Harvey, 2011), they also enabled more personal reflections by participants. In addition, they gave the researcher insight into couples' otherwise private 'couple lexes' (Gabb, 2008, p. 141), illustrating how they framed and made personal sense of encounters. Participants were offered the choice of producing either handwritten or electronic format diaries. With 'hard to reach' couples and/or those with limited literacy skills, diaries were completed retrospectively in dialogue with the researcher, in verbal format. Rather than adhere to the structured diurnal accounts that characterise time-use diary methods (Bolger, Davis, & Rafaeli, 2003; Gershuny & Sullivan, 1998), our diary format was extremely flexible and participants included photos and sketches as well as mementos of time spent together.

Participants were, however, given clear guidelines on the kinds of experiences that they might write about in their diaries. These included time and activities spent together and apart from a partner; actions or words that had resulted in reflection about the relationship in some way; one good moment in each day and one challenging experience. These suggestions did not aim to delimit the scope of interactions that were included but were designed to ensure that we generated information on everyday relationship practices and experiences rather than highly charged or unusually significant events. Completed diaries were then discussed in the follow-up interview alongside emotion maps.

The individual interviews were in two halves. In the first half, participants were invited to talk freely about experiences and different relationships across their life. This non-directive interview approach drew on methods advanced in psycho-social research (Hollway & Jefferson, 2000; Wengraf, 2001) and we thus posed the same single open question

Figure A1.1 Emoticons

to all participants: 'Tell us about your relationship: how does it work?' Researchers listened attentively to what was said and resisted making interventions which might steer the course of the interview. During the second half of the interview participants were invited to talk through the events and experiences described in their diary and depicted on the emotion map.

Couple interviews were structured around discussion of a series of collages which had been pre-prepared by the research team. Here, couples were asked to reflect on how the depicted scenarios connected with or diverged from their personal experience of, and/or opinions about, the meanings of long-term relationships. The collages addressed our central research themes and included relationship work (such as household chores, gestures and gifts); physical affection and sex; children and childhoods; money; 'significant others' (such as friends, family, in-laws, pets, faith community); social policy and welfare; and media representations. The method was also used as a participatory technique with small groups of participants attending local community centres in socially disadvantaged neighbourhoods. In this context, collages were produced by the groups from a range of media materials provided by the researcher, whose field notes, in turn, generated ethnographic data. Both collage techniques were designed to facilitate new ways of 'seeing' (Fink & Lomax, 2012), interrogating the management of public–private boundaries (Gabb, 2013) and how cultural meanings and personal experience of couple relationships intersected.

Our practices approach proved to be highly effective for this study of couples in long-term relationships. A focus on the everyday and ordinariness evinced the different ways, at different times and in different emotional and geographical spaces, that relationships were experienced, understood and rendered meaningful. Our research design also encouraged reflexivity. Participants' accounts were often highly disclosing and deeply personal. Most volunteered that the research experience had been a positive intervention, providing a pause for reflection in what were typically busy work–personal lives. This goes some way to explaining why, despite the significant commitment required from participants to the fieldwork, research attrition tended to happen at the point of recruitment rather than mid-process. The study offered participants 'time out' to 'look in', affording the couple an opportunity to redress issues and, just as importantly, a breathing space that allowed them to appreciate their partner and the things they valued about their relationship. We do not, however, perceive the interview exchange to have been a therapeutic encounter (Laslett & Rapport, 1975); instead, we situate it within the context of psycho-social research which has suggested that it may be 'reassuring and therapeutic to talk' about deeply personal or even troubling experience (Hollway & Jefferson, 2000, pp. 86–87). Research participation thus facilitated a critical intervention rather than therapeutic imitation or 'faked friendship' (Duncombe & Jessop, 2002). Couples expressed their thanks at being listened to and heard; we, as a research team, remain humbled and immensely grateful for the trust invested in us.

Appendix 2: Tables

Table A2.1 'What does your partner do for you that makes you feel appreciated?' All participants (UK)

Items coded	All women (% and rank)		Mothers (% and rank)		Childless women (% and rank)		All men (% and rank)		Fathers (% and rank)		Childless men (% and rank)	
Says thank you and/or gives me compliments	13.7	1	14.3	1	12.7	1	11.1	1	10.5	1	12	1
Gives me cards, gift, flowers, etc.	8.5	2	9	3	7.7	6	6.4	8	6	9	6.8	8
Does/shares the household chores and/or childcare	8	3	9.6	2	5.7	9	4.5	10	6.1	8	2.1	14
Talks with me and listens to me	7.8	4	6.5	5	9.9	2	7.8	5	7.5	5	8.1	4
Is physically affectionate	7.7	5	6.5	6	9.4	3	7.7	6	7.3	6	9.9	2

(continued)

© The Author(s) 2018
J. Gabb, J. Fink, *Couple Relationships in the 21st Century*, Palgrave Macmillan Studies in Family and Intimate Life, DOI 10.1007/978-3-319-59698-3

Table A2.1 (continued)

Items coded	All women (% and rank)		Mothers (% and rank)		Childless women (% and rank)		All men (% and rank)		Fathers (% and rank)		Childless men (% and rank)	
Says and/or shows s/he loves me	7.3	6	6.6	7	8.2	5	7.7	7	7.3	7	7	6
Cooks some/all of our meals	7.3	7	6.2	8	8.4	4	8.1	4	9.4	3	6.2	9
Makes kind and thoughtful gestures	6.4	8	5.6	9	7.7	7	6.3	9	5.7	10	7	7
Makes me tea/ coffee and/or breakfast in bed	6.2	9	7.4	4	4.3	11	1.2	15	1.3	15	1	15
Supports and looks after me	5.7	10	5.4	10	6.1	8	9.1	2	9.9	2	7.9	5
Is always there for me	4.2	11	3.8	11	4.8	10	8.5	3	7.9	4	9.5	3
Values me and respects my opinions	3	12	3.2	12	2.7	12	3.8	11	4.1	11	3.1	12
Makes time to be together, as a couple	2.1	13	1.7	14	2.6	13	2.6	13	1.6	14	3.5	10
Supports my personal interests/career	2.1	14	2.5	13	1.4	14	3.4	12	3.4	12	3.3	11
Sexual intimacy	0.7	15	0.7	15	0.8	15	2.6	14	2.4	13	2.9	13
Others	9.3		11		7.6		9.2		9.6		9.7	
Total	100		100		100		100		100		100	

Table A2.2 'What do you like best about your relationship?' All participants (UK)

Items coded	All women (% and rank)		Mothers (% and rank)		Childless women (% and rank)		All men (% and rank)		Fathers (% and rank)		Childless men (% and rank)	
Laughing together	12.1	1	11.8	1	12.7	1	7.0	6	5.6	8	9.0	4
Sharing values and interests	10.9	2	11.5	2	10.0	2	12.2	1	12.7	1	11.5	1
Being best friends	8.5	3	9.0	3	7.7	4	10.0	2	9.8	2	10.5	2
Being cared for and feeling supported	7.8	4	7.9	5	7.4	5	7.2	5	6.6	5	8.0	5
Feeling safe and secure	7.3	5	8.2	4	5.7	9	5.8	8	5.2	9	6.5	7
Being happy	6.7	7	5.5	7	8.7	3	7.7	4	6.7	4	9.2	3
Trust	6.7	6	6.9	6	6.3	6	5.9	7	6.5	6	5.0	10
Sharing a close relationship	5.3	8	4.9	9	6.0	8	8.0	3	8.1	3	7.8	6
Talking and listening	5.1	9	4.4	10	6.3	7	3.8	11	3.2	13	4.8	11
Being in love and/or being loved	5.0	10	5.2	8	4.6	11	5.2	9	5.1	10	5.3	9
Physical affection	4.3	11	3.4	12	5.7	10	3.8	12	2.7	15	5.5	8
Spending time together	3.8	12	3.2	13	4.6	12	3.7	13	4.4	12	2.9	13
Being a family and/or having children	2.8	13	4.5	11	0.1	15	3.7	14	6.2	7	0.0	15
We support each other	2.4	14	2.3	14	2.7	14	2.8	15	3.2	14	2.1	14
Sexual intimacy	2.4	15	2.2	15	2.8	13	4.8	10	5.0	11	4.6	12
Others	8.9		9.1		8.7		8.4		9.0		7.3	
Total	100		100		100		100		100		100	

Table A2.3 'What do you like least about your relationship?' All participants (UK)

Items coded	All Women (% and rank)		Mothers (% and rank)		Childless women (% and rank)		All men (% and rank)		Fathers (% and rank)		Childless men (% and rank)	
Poor communication	8.9	1	9	1	8.7	1	6.6	4	5	8	8.8	3
Arguments and/ or conflicts	8.3	2	8.2	2	8.4	2	11.1	1	11.7	1	10.1	1
Housework and/ or childcare are not shared fairly	7.5	3	7	5	8.3	3	5	8	5.2	7	4.7	10
Issues with balancing work and home life	7	4	7.1	4	7	4	6.4	6	6.6	4	5.8	7
Few shared values and/or interests	6.7	5	6.9	6	6.5	6	7.1	3	5.8	5	9.2	2
Not enough couple time	6.7	6	7.4	3	5.5	8	6.5	5	7.4	3	5.4	8
Money issues	6.4	7	6.4	7	6.5	7	5.3	7	4.9	9	6.1	6
Living apart and/or housing issues	5	8	3.7	12	7	5	4.7	10	3.5	10	6.3	4
Different needs/ expectations around sexual intimacy	4.2	9	3.8	11	5	9	8.1	2	9.3	2	6.3	5
Lack of closeness	4.1	10	4.4	8	3.7	10	3.4	13	3.4	11	3.4	13
Partner's undesirable personality traits	3.9	11	4	10	3.4	12	3.6	12	3.1	12	4.5	11
Annoying habits	3.6	12	4.1	9	2.8	15	2.2	14	2.4	14	2	14
Issues with partner's friends or family	3.4	13	3.4	13	3.5	11	3.7	11	2.8	13	5.2	9
Nothing	3.1	14	3.1	14	3.2	14	4.9	9	5.8	6	3.6	12
Trust issues	2.8	15	2.4	15	3.4	13	1.8	15	1.9	15	1.6	15
Others	18.4		19.1		17.1		19.6		21.2		17	
Total	100		100		100		100		100		100	

Table A2.4 'Who is the most important person in your life?' Gender and parenthood by age of youngest child

	Child under 5 years (%)	Child 5–9 years old (%)	Child 10–17 years old (%)	Child aged 18 and over (%)
Mothers selecting child/ren	75	78	64	40
Fathers selecting child/ren	59	47	35	9
Mothers selecting partner	21	19	30	55
Fathers selecting partner	38	52	57	89

Table A2.5 'My partner wants to have sex more often than I do' by gender and parenthood

	Strongly disagree (%)	Disagree (%)	Neither agree nor disagree (%)	Agree (%)	Strongly agree (%)
Fathers	25.00	44.10	21.20	8.50	1.10
Childless men	18.90	38.70	25.90	9.70	6.70
Mothers	9.80	26.60	23.30	30.40	9.90
Childless women	12.80	33.20	24.00	22.40	7.60

Table A2.6 'My partner wants to have sex more often than I do' by relationship status and residency

	Strongly disagree (%)	Disagree (%)	Neither agree nor disagree (%)	Agree (%)	Strongly agree (%)
Married	11.90	29.60	24.60	26.00	7.90
Civil partnership	17.00	35.50	24.10	16.30	7.10
Cohabiting	13.90	32.50	20.70	23.40	9.50
Living apart together (LAT)	19.00	36.20	22.30	17.20	5.30
Going out with someone	11.70	44.20	22.10	11.70	10.40

Table A2.7 'My partner wants to have sex more often than I do' by parenthood and sexuality

	Strongly disagree (%)	Disagree (%)	Neither agree nor disagree (%)	Agree (%)	Strongly agree (%)
LGBQ childfree couples	18.60	37.60	22.80	15.10	5.90
LGBQ parents	21.30	35.60	20.20	17.00	5.90
Heterosexual childfree couples	13.00	33.10	24.70	21.30	7.90
Heterosexual parents	12.20	29.40	23.20	26.80	8.40

Table A2.8 Means and Standard Deviations for relationship measures by gender and parenting status

	Childfree women		Mothers		Childfree men		Fathers	
	Mean	SD	Mean	SD	Mean	SD	Mean	SD
Relationship quality	4.22	0.54	4.01	0.68	4.20	0.53	4.03	0.67
Relationship with partner	4.08	0.61	3.82	0.75	4.06	0.60	3.89	0.73
Relationship maintenance	4.19	0.56	3.83	0.71	4.16	0.52	3.84	0.71
Happiness with relationship/ partner	4.45	0.72	4.24	0.89	4.47	0.66	4.36	0.82
Happiness with life	4.03	0.79	4.12	0.79	4.05	0.77	4.04	0.81

Table A2.9 Composition of survey sample

		%	Numbers
Gender	Male	19.0	856
	Female	80.4	3613
	Other/missing	0.6	25
Sexual orientation	Heterosexual	86.5	3886
	Gay/lesbian	6.0	268
	Bisexual	5.5	246
	Other/not disclosed	2.0	94
Relationship status	Married	59.7	2685
	Civil partnership	2.8	124
	Living together	24.3	1090
	Living apart together (LAT)	11.1	501
	Going out with someone	1.6	70
	Other/not disclosed	0.5	24
Age	16–24; 25–34 (younger)	36.1	1621
	35–44; 45–54 (middle)	44.6	2004
	55–64; 65+ (older)	19.1	858
	Not disclosed	0.2	11
Educational qualifications	Alevels, voc. quals and below	26.7	[1]199
	UG, PG and prof. quals	70.6	3174
	Other/not disclosed	2.7	121
Religion	Religion: Yes	44.3	[1]991
	Religion: No	50.3	[22]59
	Other/not disclosed	5.4	[2]44
Children	Parents (children living with/ left home)	60.4	2715
	Childless	37.8	1696
	Not disclosed	1.8	83
Ethnicity	White	91.1	4095
	BME/mixed race	5.7	[2]53
	Not disclosed	3.2	146
Total			4494

Bibliography

Bolger, N., Davis, A., & Rafaeli, E. (2003). Diary Methods: Capturing Life as It Is Lived. *Annual Review of Psychology, 54*(1), 579–616.

Bucerius, S. M. (2013). Becoming a 'Trusted Outsider': Gender, Ethnicity, and Inequality in Ethnographic Research. *Journal of Contemporary Ethnography, 42*(6), 690–721.

Duncombe, J., & Jessop, J. (2002). Doing Rapport and the Ethics of Faking Friendship. In M. Mauthner, M. Birch, J. Jessop, & T. Miller (Eds.), *Ethics in Qualitative Research* (pp. 107–123). London: Sage.

Evangelou, M., Coxon, K., Sylva, K., Smith, S., & Chan, L. L. S. (2013). Seeking to Engage 'Hard-to-Reach' Families: Towards a Transferable Model of Intervention. *Children & Society, 27*(2), 127–138.

Fink, J., & Gabb, J. (2014). Configuring Generations: Cross-Disciplinary Perspectives. *Families, Relationships and Societies, 3*(3), 1–6.

Fink, J., & Lomax, H. (2012). Introduction: Inequalities, Images and Insights for Policy and Research. *Critical Social Policy, 32*(1), 3–10.

Fuss, D. (1991). *Inside/Out. Lesbian Theories, Gay Theories*. New York: Routledge.

Gabb, J. (2004). Critical Differentials: Querying the Contrarieties between Research on Lesbian Parent Families. *Sexualities, 7*(2), 171–187.

Gershuny, J., & Sullivan, O. (1998). The Sociological Uses of Time-Use Diary Analysis. *European Sociological Review, 14*(1), 69–85.

© The Author(s) 2018
J. Gabb, J. Fink, *Couple Relationships in the 21st Century*, Palgrave Macmillan Studies in Family and Intimate Life, DOI 10.1007/978-3-319-59698-3

Harvey, L. (2011). Intimate Reflections: Private Diaries in Qualitative Research. *Qualitative Research, 11*(6), 664–682.

Hollway, W., & Jefferson, T. (2000). *Doing Qualitative Research Differently: Free Association, Narrative and the Interview Method.* London, Thousand Oaks, and New Delhi: Sage Publications.

Laslett, B., & Rapport, R. (1975). Collaborative Interviewing and Interactive Research. *Journal of Marriage and the Family, 37,* 968–977.

Nilsen, A. & Brannen, J. (2014). An Intergenerational Approach to Transitions to Adulthood: The Importance of History and Biography. *Sociological Research Online, 19*(2). Retrieved from; http://www.socresonline.org.uk/19/12/19.html

Wacquant, L. (2008). *Urban Outcasts: A Comparative Sociology of Advanced Marginality.* Cambridge: Polity Press.

Wengraf, T. (2001). *Qualitative Research Interviewing: Biographic Narrative and Semi-structured Method.* London: Sage.

Index

© The Author(s) 2018
J. Gabb, J. Fink, *Couple Relationships in the 21st Century*, Palgrave Macmillan Studies
in Family and Intimate Life, DOI 10.1007/978-3-319-59698-3

Printed by Printforce, the Netherlands